George William Childs

The Public ledger building, Philadelphia

George William Childs

The Public ledger building, Philadelphia

ISBN/EAN: 9783741182099

Manufactured in Europe, USA, Canada, Australia, Japa

Cover: Foto ©Thomas Meinert / pixelio.de

Manufactured and distributed by brebook publishing software (www.brebook.com)

George William Childs

The Public ledger building, Philadelphia

Geo. W. Childs

THE

PUBLIC LEDGER BUILDING,

PHILADELPHIA:

WITH AN

ACCOUNT OF THE PROCEEDINGS

CONNECTED WITH ITS

OPENING JUNE 20, 1867.

PHILADELPHIA:
GEORGE W. CHILDS.
1868.

CONTENTS.

	PAGE
THE NEW LEDGER BUILDING	3
The Ledger Building	6
The Exterior View	8
The Ground Plan	15
The Publication Office	16
The Press Room	23
The Composing Room	28
The Stereotype Foundry	31
Editorial Rooms	31
The Job Printing Office	33
The Book Publication Office	34
The Stores	85
The Offices	36
Access to the Rooms	38
The Water Supply	39
General Details	39
OPENING OF THE NEW LEDGER BUILDING	43
Remarks of Hon. Charles Gilpin	46
Remarks of Mr. John McArthur, Jr., Architect	48
Remarks of Hon. Daniel M. Fox	50
Remarks of Mr. Wm. V. McKean	51
BANQUET AT THE CONTINENTAL HOTEL	57
Prayer of Bishop Simpson	59
Address of Mayor McMichael	60
Remarks of Hon. Joseph R. Chandler, LL.D.	63
Remarks of Mayor Hoffman, of New York	69
Remarks of General Meade	73
Remarks of Gen. Robeson, of New Jersey	79

(v)

CONTENTS.

BANQUET AT THE CONTINENTAL HOTEL—continued. PAGE
   Remarks of Hon. James Brooks, of New York . . . 80
   Remarks of Hon. J. J. Stewart, of Maryland . . . 83
   Remarks of Paul B. Du Chaillu, the African Explorer . 88
   Remarks of Hon. Wm. D. Kelley 90
   Remarks of Rev. Dr. Hall, of Dublin, Ireland . . . 93
   Remarks of Gen. Hiram Walbridge, of New York . . 94
   Remarks of Mr. George H. Stuart, of Philadelphia . . 97
   Tribute to Anthony J. Drexel, Esq. 98
      Remarks of Mr. W. V. McKean 98
      Remarks of Mr. George H. Stuart 99

FOURTH OF JULY ENTERTAINMENT TO THE LEDGER EMPLOYES . . . 102
   Address of Mr. McKean 103
   Remarks of Mr. Nicholson 108
   Remarks of Mr. Muckle 111
   Remarks of Mr. Drane 112
   The Newsboys' Banquet 116
   Employer and Employed 117
   Remarks of Joseph Sailer, Esq. 118

CORRESPONDENCE 121
   His Excellency Andrew Johnson, President of the United States . . . 123
   Hon. William H. Seward, Secretary of State of the United States . . . 124
   Hon. Gideon Welles, Secretary of the Navy . . . 124
   Hon. Edwin M. Stanton, Secretary of War . . . 125
   Hon. Millard Fillmore, Ex-President of the United States . 125
   General Grant 126
   Chief Justice Chase to Dr. Elder 126
   Hon. S. P. Chase, LL.D., Chief Justice of the Supreme Court of the United States . . . 127
   Hon. W. Dennison, late Postmaster-General of the United States . . . 127
   Major-General Geary, Governor of Pennsylvania . . 128
   Hon. Marcus L. Ward, Governor of New Jersey . . 130
   Major-General Schenck, Member of Congress from Ohio . 130
   Hon. Thomas Swann, Governor of Maryland . . . 131
   Hon. Simon Cameron, U. S. Senator from Pennsylvania . 132

CORRESPONDENCE—*continued.* PAGE

General C. E. Phelps, Member of Congress from Baltimore City 132
George S. Hillard, LL. D., United States District Attorney for Massachusetts 134
Hon. A. G. Cattell, United States Senator from New Jersey 134
Major-General Chamberlain, Governor of Maine 135
Hon. Reverdy Johnson, LL. D., United States Senator from Maryland 135
Commodore Turner, United States Navy 136
Hon. A. H. Rice, Member of Congress from Massachusetts and Ex-Mayor of Boston 137
Rear-Admiral Charles Stewart, United States Navy 138
Dr. Oliver Wendell Holmes 139
Ralph Waldo Emerson, Esq. 140
Henry Wadsworth Longfellow, the Poet 140
Hon. George Bancroft, LL. D., the Historian 141
Francis Lieber, LL. D., Professor in Columbia College, New York 141
Hon. Robert C. Winthrop, LL. D., of Massachusetts 142
Major-General Patterson 142
Professor Joseph Henry, LL. D., Secretary of the Smithsonian Institution, Washington, D. C. 143
Stephen Colwell, LL. D., Author of various works on Political Economy 143
George William Curtis, Esq. 144
Henry T. Tuckerman, Esq., the Essayist 145
Jas. Parton, Esq., Author of the Lives of Franklin, Aaron Burr, Andrew Jackson, &c. 145
Henry C. Carey, LL. D., the well-known writer on Political Economy 146
Rev. William R. Alger 146
Rev. Henry Ward Beecher 146
Epes Sargent, Esq., the Author 147
S. Austin Allibone, LL. D., Author of the "Dictionary of Authors and Literature" 148
Rev. E. H. Chapin, D. D. 149
Rev. T. F. Curtis, D. D., late Professor in the University of Lewisburg, Pa. 150
Rev. M. Simpson, D. D., Bishop of the Methodist Episcopal Church 151
Rev. C. P. Krauth, D. D., Norton Professor of Theology in the Theological Seminary of the Evangelical Lutheran Church in Philadelphia 152

CONTENTS.

CORRESPONDENCE—continued. PAGE

Rev. J. P. Thompson, D. D., Pastor of Tabernacle Church, New York City 153
Hon. Emory Washburn, LL. D., Ex-Governor of Massachusetts, and Resident Professor of Law at Harvard University 154
Henry Coppée, LL. D., President of the Lehigh University, Pa. 155
Professor C. W. Shields, D. D. 156
M. L. Stœver, Professor in Pennsylvania College 157
Hon. John H. B. Latrobe 157
Dr. Hammond, late Surgeon-General in the U. S. Army 157
George H. Boker, Secretary of the Union League of Philadelphia 158
Hon. George W. Woodward, LL. D., Chief-Justice of the Supreme Court of Pennsylvania 159
Hon. George Sharswood, LL. D., President Judge of the District Court of Philadelphia 159
J. I. Clark Hare, Associate Justice of the District Court of Philadelphia 160
Joseph Harrison, M. E. 162
George S. Appleton, Esq. (D. Appleton & Co., Publishers), New York 163
W. B. Dinsmore, President of the Adams Express Company 163
Col. R. M. Hoe, Inventor of Hoe's celebrated Printing-Presses 164
R. Dunglison, M. D., Professor in the Jefferson Medical College, Philadelphia 165
General E. S. Sanford, late President of the American Telegraph Company 166
Harper & Brothers, Publishers, New York 167
John Walter, Esq., M. P., Proprietor of the "London Times" 168
J. T. Fields, Esq. (Ticknor & Fields, Publishers), Boston 168
Theodore Tilton, Esq., Editor of "The Independent" 169
Rev. Wm. M. Engles, D. D., Editor of "The Presbyterian" 169
George P. Putnam, Esq., Publisher, New York 170
Dr. J. G. Holland (Timothy Titcomb), the well-known Author 173
Rev. Dr. Crooks, Editor of "The Methodist" 173
Col. Greene, Editor of the "Boston Post" 174
E. P. Whipple, Esq. 174

CONTENTS.   ix

CORRESPONDENCE—*continued*.   PAGE

Editors and Proprietors of the "Journal of Commerce,"
    New York 173
F. D. Penniman, Esq., Editor of the "Pittsburgh Gazette" 175
R. Shelton Mackenzie, D. C. L. 175
M. Halstead, Esq., Editor and Proprietor of the "Cincin-
    nati Commercial" 176
Horace Greeley, Editor of the "New York Tribune" . 177
Joshua Leavitt, Esq., "New York Evening Post" . . 178
Col. A. J. H. Duganne, Editor of the "New York Dispatch" 179
Hon. Wm. Bross, Lieutenant-Governor of Illinois, and one
    of the Proprietors and Editors of the "Chicago Tribune" 180
C. D. Brigham, Editor of the "Pittsburgh Commercial" . 181
The Editors and Proprietors of the "Missouri Republican" 182
A. M. Holbrook, Esq., Proprietor and Editor of the New
    Orleans "Picayune" 183
W. A. Collins, Esq., Editor of the "Pittsburgh Chronicle" 184
S. M. Pettengill, Esq. 185
Col. John S. Dusolle, Editor of the "New York Sunday
    Times" 185
L. A. Godey, Esq., Editor and Proprietor of the "Lady's
    Book" 186

The New Ledger Building.

THE NEW LEDGER BUILDING.

The removal of the PUBLIC LEDGER ESTABLISHMENT from the building so long occupied by its offices and workrooms gives occasion for a description of the new building now devoted to its uses. And first it will be in order to say something concerning the removal itself. Twenty-five years ago the vicinity of Third and Chestnut Streets had become, and seemed likely to remain, the business centre of Philadelphia for the next fifty years. The situation of the Post-Office, the Custom House, the Merchants' Exchange, the United States Bank, the bankers' and brokers' offices, and some of the principal Banks, Insurance Companies' offices, the mercantile and commercial quarters, and most of the newspaper offices, gave occasion to nearly every person engaged in active business to pass that corner several times every day. This being the situation of affairs, the founders of the PUBLIC LEDGER selected that business centre as the proper locality for the Publication Office of the great popular newspaper of Philadelphia. They selected the southwest corner of the junction of those two streets, and having secured two lots, with a frontage of about fifty feet on Chestnut, with nearly the same depth on Third Street, they erected upon it buildings covering the whole ground plan, and six stories in height. These capacious quarters they anticipated would be equal to any future demands for space that were likely to occur to any newspaper in Philadelphia, and there the PUBLIC LEDGER ESTABLISH-

MENT remained until June, 1867. Prior to that date, however, two of the principal Government offices had been removed a few hundred yards westward, and some of the heavy business of the city had taken the same direction; and the commodious building that was thought to be equal to any exigency that might ever arise in the history of the paper was found to be altogether insufficient for the uses of the PUBLIC LEDGER. For several years past the greatly expanded business of the establishment has demanded additional room, and the rapid execution of its daily work has been somewhat retarded on that account. This was clear to the present proprietor when he purchased the PUBLIC LEDGER from its founders, and even at the time when negotiations were going on for purchasing the newspaper, Mr. Childs saw that it would be necessary to change its quarters at the earliest possible opportunity. He accordingly fixed in his mind the southwest corner of Sixth and Chestnut Streets as a suitable locality for the New Publication Office, and immediately upon the purchase of the paper commenced the preliminaries for obtaining the large lot of ground upon that corner. The purchase of the several lots of ground that now form the site of the NEW LEDGER BUILDING, and the erection of that spacious edifice itself, are therefore but the carrying out of a resolve that was made at the same time the paper was purchased.

Few persons who peruse their morning papers at the breakfast table, winter and summer, in sunshine and storm, think of the amount of capital invested, the labor involved, and the care and anxiety incident to the preparation and publication of the sheet which is so regularly served at all seasons of the year. Even in the newspaper world, surrounded as we are by all the appliances of the business, we sometimes ignore that which makes the daily journal a success, and we frequently overlook the steady progress made and still making in improving the machinery and general organization of a first-class daily newspaper establishment. Accustomed now to the appearance and use of "Hoe's Last Fast," the old and cumbersome hand-press of a hundred years ago is forgotten, and it seems like a romance to read of Bradford's successful effort, in 1719, to publish the first newspaper in Pennsylvania, when muscle, not steam, was the motive power that drove the lumbering wooden structure denominated a press, and which required days for the work accomplished now in minutes. The changes in newspaper machinery have been so rapid, and so varied, that it is almost impossible to follow the successive displays of American ingenuity. We, therefore, are content to accept the present as the only proper type of the newspaper business. But it is not our purpose to trace the history of newspaper enterprise, however interesting and instructive it might prove. It is with the present we deal, and in the accompanying sketch of the most extensive and complete newspaper establishment in Europe or America, we shall aim to convey a slight idea of one of the most striking improvements in Philadelphia, and at the same time indicate to what perfection newspaper machinery and journalistic organization have been brought in 1867.

As the originator, constant advocate, and steadfast friend of every great improvement that has marked the progress of Philadelphia for the past thirty years, it was natural that the PUBLIC LEDGER should take one more step in advance, and, while furnishing to the city a magnificent structure, architecturally considered, secure at the same time for itself a building which, in everything required for the prompt, speedy, and convenient transaction of the business incident to the publication of a first-class daily paper, is without an equal in the world. To those of us who have watched the gradual rise of the new LEDGER BUILDING, and are familiar with every detail of its construction, its immense size, as well as entire adaptability to the purposes designed, is apparent. But it is not so easy in a printed description to convey the same idea to the reader. Much of the building is concealed from the public view, and in admiring the imposing appearance of the structure as viewed from the street, the spectator can be expected only to appreciate that which is visible, appealing only to his sense of the beautiful and ornamental, without taking heed of the endless details of the interior. In the accompanying sketch, therefore, we shall seek to give merely the dimensions, figures, and such prominent features as may enable those interested to secure at least a partial conception of the magnitude, architectural beauty, and general completeness of the establishment at the southwest corner of Sixth and Chestnut Streets, to be hereafter known as

THE LEDGER BUILDING.

The first step made by the present proprietor of the LEDGER was to secure, by purchase, the structure on the southwest corner of Sixth and Chestnut Streets, eighty-four feet on Chestnut and seventy-nine feet on Sixth, erected in 1854, and known as the Howell Building. Originally, without alterations and improvements, it was not considered an imposing structure. Large as it was, it was deemed too contracted, and the determination was at once formed to add not only to its proportions and appearance, but to so alter the interior as to radically change its appearance, and better fit it for the use of the LEDGER, and for the transaction of business in the job printing office. There were considerations of space, ventilation, light, and easy access to the various stories and apartments involved. By the extensive purchases of adjoining property on Sixth Street, Mr. JOHN McARTHUR, Jr., the architect, assisted by Mr. Childs, was enabled to arrange a plan complete in all these requisites. Not only were the additions to the property on Sixth Street purchased with reference to the needs of the PUBLIC LEDGER and its appurtenances, but at the same time the acquisition of ground allowed the architect to give to the property on Chestnut Street a rear outlet, as well as ample light and ventilation, features neglected necessarily in the original construction of the Howell Buildings. The last of these purchases was consummated late in the summer of 1865. The contract for the entire improvement was awarded to Mr. R. J. Dobbins, the well-known builder, of Philadelphia. On the 1st of May, 1866, Mr. Dobbins commenced work under the contract. At the outset, the old structures on Sixth Street, south of the main building, were torn down, and extensive excavations twenty feet below the pavement were made for the basement, especially designed as the Press Room of the LEDGER. This portion of the work, as well as the entire construction of the new building, and the alterations to the old, was carefully and constantly superintended by the architect, Mr. McArthur, and his able assistant Mr. George Summers, both of whom exercised every possible precaution in order that the details of the specifications in the contract should be complied with in every respect. During the temporary absence of Mr. McArthur in Mexico, the responsibility rested entirely upon Mr. Summers, who has acquitted himself with entire satisfaction to all who are interested in the building. It is hardly necessary to say that in this building Mr. McArthur has but achieved another triumph, and added another to the many important architectural structures with which his skill and taste as an architect have enabled him to beautify and adorn Philadelphia. The work progressed steadily through the spring, summer, and autumn of 1866, and by the approach of winter the new portions were under roof and partially plastered. The introduction of boilers in the Press Room, and the distribution of pipe throughout the building, allowed the work to be forwarded during the cold weather, and on the 20th of June, 1867, the building was ready for its occupants.

THE EXTERIOR VIEW.

As soon as the excavations were made, substantial foundation walls, laid with the best stone, in approved hydraulic cement and mortar, were built, and upon the solid basis thus prepared granite and Iron were piled until the level of the sidewalk was reached. The building erected upon this foundation, viewed from the exterior, presents a splendid brownstone structure, eighty-four feet on Chestnut Street and one hundred and sixty-five on Sixth Street, five stories in height, with a Mansard roof. The architectural plan of the Howell Building was followed in the additions, so far as outward appearances are concerned, thus giving to each story, above the first, a series of brownstone piers or pilasters to mark the divisions between the windows. Between each story the ornamentation in stone is simple and chaste, consisting mainly of arches over the heads of the windows, with carved keystones and cornice, frieze and architrave, as a relief to what might otherwise be the monotony of one hundred and sixteen windows above the first story on Sixth Street, and fifty-six windows on Chestnut Street, or one hundred and seventy-two windows on the two fronts. In the middle of the Sixth Street front there is a slight projection, running the height of the elevation. This tends still further to vary the architectural design. The first story is composed of heavy wrought iron columns, painted and sanded in imitation of brownstone, supporting the stonework above. No less than one hundred and sixty-seven tons of iron were used in the construction of these columns. They are forty-two in number, and give forty-one openings for the doors and windows for the first story on the two main fronts. The doors and windows in the stores on Chestnut Street, occupied by A. T. Stewart & Co., of New York, and Cadbury, Rhoads & Thomas, of Philadelphia, as well as those of two stores on Sixth Street, are provided with wrought iron rolling shutters of Johnson's pattern, twenty-five in number, furnished by the Architectural Iron Works of New York. The whole of these, including slats, grooves, weights, boxes, shafting, crank stands, and chain, weigh twenty-eight thousand four hundred pounds.

COAT-OF-ARMS OF PENNSYLVANIA.

Over the main doorway of the Sixth Street front, about the centre of the building, is placed the coat-of-arms of Pennsylvania, carved in light Brunswick stone, from an elaborate design by BAILLY, the sculptor, at the establishment of Struthers & Son, the well-known marble workers. The whole design occupies a space eight feet in length and five in height, the horses being half the natural size. On the base a band contains the inscription "PUBLIC LEDGER," and also the monogram "G. W. C." The design is exceedingly bold, and has been executed with skill and taste.

The corner of Sixth and Chestnut Streets contains a still more striking figure. Upon a stone column, two feet six inches in diameter and eighteen feet in height, set against the angle of the building, stands the statue of Franklin, cut from Brunswick stone. The figure is ten feet six inches in height, and is not only perfect in its details, but the face is said by good judges to be the best likeness of the philosopher ever carved in stone. While Bailly, the artist, was

10   THE PUBLIC LEDGER BUILDING.

engaged in modelling the figure, he was permitted by the late Mr. William J. Duane (who married a granddaughter of Franklin), to use a portrait of the printer and philosopher, painted in Paris by Duplessis, the celebrated miniature painter. This is the best likeness in existence, and the artist has succeeded well in transferring it to stone. The figure stands erect, the left hand resting upon a pedestal formed by a pile of books to the rear of the statue. The right arm is elevated, and the hand grasps the lightning-rod, while resting against the books is the traditional kite. The figure is clothed with the costume so familiar to us in the engravings of Franklin. The column upon which the statue stands is handsomely fluted, and has an ornate cap, around the neck of which is inscribed,

1836.   PUBLIC LEDGER.   1866.

STATUE OF FRANKLIN.

The front of the column contains the bulletin-board. As it stands, the top of the statue reaches to the third-story floor, and an arrangement is made by means of which, at night, the four prongs of the lightning-rod will emit flames of gaslight. At the base of the column two ornate white marble drinking fountains have been placed for the accommodation of the public. These fountains are on the face of the column about four feet from the pavement, and are of new design. Each is in the form of a lion's head, elaborately carved, and so fashioned that the head, with the water issuing from the mouth, has below it a basin for the waste; the whole being cut from one piece of marble. Set against the brownstone, the white marble forms an attractive feature of the establishment. A substantial bronze railing encircles the fountains. In the summer months, it will be one of the most welcome landmarks in Philadelphia, as the arrangement of the coiled pipe supplying the water is designed to furnish ice water at all times. The whole of this work, together with the entire dressed brownstone of the buildings, is from the establishment of STRUTHERS & SON, who set up the stone front on Sixth Street in the short space of three weeks and four days.

DRINKING FOUNTAIN.

The addition of the Mansard roof greatly increases the architectural effect of the whole structure. Without this roof the building has an elevation of sixty feet from the pavement to the elaborate stone cornice that marks the

12   THE PUBLIC LEDGER BUILDING.

line at the top, according to the original design. This roof is rendered still more attractive by being arranged with domes at the corners fifteen feet in height (from cornice), while the central elevation on Sixth Street is a dome twenty-one feet in height. The other portions of the roof are twelve feet above the cornice. Covered with slate cut ornamentally, the Mansard roof gives an appearance of increased height to the building to correspond with the long line of one hundred and sixty-five feet on Sixth Street. In front of the central dome, and as a continuation of the Sixth Street elevation, is a splendid design in brownstone, carved by Struthers & Son, from models prepared by Bailly.

CENTRAL DOME.

The entire weight of this ornament is twenty-five tons. It is in the form of a half circle, the interior face, excluding the elaborate cornice, being fourteen feet long at the base, and seven feet in height at the centre. It rises above a pedestal thirty feet long and four feet high, while the cornice that follows the curve of the circle adds three feet to the height, making a total of fourteen feet from the cornice of the building to the top of the circle. The circle is also flanked with ornamental scroll-work at the point of union with the pedestal. The face of the pedestal contains, in large block letters and figures, the inscription: "1836. PUBLIC LEDGER. 1866." The face of the half circle has sculptured upon it, in relief, a globe, four feet in diameter, with Europe and America marked on its surface. Above this, resting in a recumbent position on the clouds surrounding the globe, is the nude figure of a boy, designed by the artist to represent Young America. This figure is five feet six inches in height, and its position is such as to enable it to reach the recording book which rests upon the top of the globe. To the left is the locomotive, and to the right the forked lightning emerging from the clouds. The effect of the whole, as viewed from below, is very striking.

Along the edge of the entire front of the roof, on Sixth Street as well as on Chestnut Street, a handsome and highly ornamental iron railing, furnished by WHITE & DEVINNEY, is placed. It varies from three to seven feet in height, and is nearly four hundred feet in length, passing as it does around the domes, in addition to the front. The panels are bronzed, with the spear heads covered with gold leaf. A large flagstaff rises from each of the domes on Sixth Street. The central staff is sixty feet above the roof, giving from the pavement to the point of the lightning-rod a distance of one hundred and fifty feet. The flagstaffs at the corners are each fifty feet in height. A handsome and large set of colors, consisting of the National, State, and City Flags, have been kindly presented by HORSTMANN & BROTHER.

The vane at the roof is a pen of six feet six inches in length, and the letters marking the points of the compass are within a radius of six feet. The gilt ball on the flagstaff is sixteen inches in diameter. The arrangement of the vane includes Gatchell's improved lightning-rod—the latter consisting of a rope of twisted copper wire, containing eighteen strands of wire, about 1.16 inch in diameter.

The central dome is especially designed as a "look-out," and to that end easy access to it has been provided. From it a grand view of the city is obtained; a panorama of rare beauty presents itself before the vision of the spectator. East, west, north, and south, for miles, every object of interest in Philadelphia is clearly discernible. Southward, the line of the Delaware and Schuylkill is distinctly marked until near the union of the two streams at League Island. Point Breeze Gas Works, the Almshouse, the County Prison, as well as hundreds of factories and foundries are in view. On the north, Girard College, Fairmount Park, the Cathedral, and scores of prominent buildings are readily distinguished. East, we have the Delaware with its shipping; and west, Mantua, and the whole region known as West Philadelphia. This "look-out" promises to be an attractive spot for those who wish to secure a bird's-eye view of Philadelphia, and, for the accommodation of visitors, seats have been arranged around the flagstaff. No signs are to be allowed to disfigure the architectural effect on either front of the building.

Three large and ornamental lamp-posts, of an entirely original design, by ROBERT WOOD & Co., are placed on both fronts of the building—one at the corner of Sixth and Chestnut Streets; one on the Chestnut Street front at the west end of the building; and the third on Sixth Street at the south end of the building. Each of these lamp-posts contains upon the base, in relief, the inscription: "1836. PUBLIC LEDGER. 1866." The tops of these lamp-posts are furnished with candelabras of an entirely new pattern in this country. On the corner of Sixth and Chestnut the post contains a cluster of seven lights, grouped in a circle of six, with the seventh as the centre piece raised a few inches above its fellows. Each light is inclosed in a globe of semi-opaque glass, two feet by fourteen inches. The other two posts contain six lights, the whole forming a neat as well as beautiful addition to the front of the building. The design of these lamps is taken from similar posts ornamenting the Boulevards of Paris. While ornamental in the highest degree they in no wise interfere with the business or utilitarian design of the entire establishment. This completes an imperfect sketch of the building, as viewed from Sixth and Chestnut Streets.

THE GROUND PLAN.

A reference to the ground plan and explanations of the uses to which the various parts of the building are put, will give the best idea of its size and magnitude. The building, as now constructed, is in the form of a letter E, the long upright of the letter being represented by the Sixth Street front of one hundred and sixty-five feet, with one projection of eighty-four feet on Chestnut, and another of one hundred and ten feet at right angles with Sixth Street, at the south end. The central projection of the letter E, at the first story, forms part of the Chestnut Street stores, but above this the arrangement of skylights at the second story of the stores enables the letter E plan to be pursued the remainder of the elevation, giving light and ventilation to all parts of the building. The middle projection, at right angles with Sixth Street, is ninety-three feet from Chestnut Street, and extends westward, eighteen feet in width, a distance of fifty-eight feet, measured above the first story. The projection at right angles with Sixth Street, at the south end, is thirty-six feet in width, extending westward one hundred and sixteen feet. This projection has two large open spaces, or "well-holes," as they are called, on the south side, each ten feet by ten feet, intended to provide light and ventilation to the wing in addition to that which is secured through the numerous windows on the north wall of this portion of the building. These well-holes extend to the basement, and thus give addition of light and ventilation to the Press Room. The stores on Chestnut Street extend one hundred and eleven feet in depth, one store being thirty-six feet front, and the other twenty-five. As before stated, the first floors of the Chestnut Street stores include the middle projection of what we have called the letter E. This brings the rear of the stores to the opening between this and the southernmost projection, the opening being a street eighteen feet in width, leading to George's Court, and thence to Sansom Street. This street, or rear outlet, is paved with heavy slabs of granite, and furnishes an easy means of access for goods to the Chestnut Street stores as well as the Press Room of the LEDGER. Above the first story the Chestnut Street stores are seventy-nine feet in depth. The pavement surrounding the two main fronts consists of heavy slabs of granite, resting upon iron girders extending from the curb to the line of the building. The circular openings in the granite, as well as the space near the entrance to the offices on Sixth Street and the stores on Chestnut Street, are fitted with Hyatt's Patent Protected Lead-band Vault Lights, thus making the basement almost as light as the upper portions of the building. The figures given above are maintained throughout the building, and in the details of the interior we shall indicate the use to which the space thus obtained is put.

THE PUBLICATION OFFICE.

First, we have the Publication Office on the first floor, at the corner, twenty-three feet on Chestnut, by sixty feet on Sixth, and fifteen feet ten inches from floor to ceiling. No business apartment anything like it has ever been constructed in America, and with the exception of a few old baronial castles and one or two libraries across the water, but little of the kind is to be seen even in Europe. The room is a marvel of delicate joinery work, and is one entire mass of dark walnut and butternut-wood, or, as it is sometimes called, white walnut. Instead of plaster, the sides

and ceiling are wainscoted with these costly woods, while
the counters, fixtures, furniture, and general appointments
are made to correspond in every respect with the elaborate
design of the architect. Butternut-wood is similar in

BUSINESS DEPARTMENT.

appearance to oak, but is of a finer grain, admitting of a
better polish and finish. The ceiling and sides of the room
are a series of panels within panels, with the two woods
distributed in such a manner as to produce the greatest
effect by the contrast in colors. The ceiling is divided into
three principal panels, nineteen feet by ten feet, with heavy

mouldings and cornice. These, again, are surrounded by a border of smaller panels, twenty-four in number, each five feet four inches by two feet eight inches.

The principal panels have subdivisions and circular centre pieces pierced for the gas fixtures and chandeliers. These chandeliers, three in number, together with the gas fixtures throughout the building, were furnished by MISKEY, MERRILL & THACKARA. Each chandelier has six lights, with ground-glass globes. They are of an original pattern, and, in design and bronze and gold finish, are made to correspond with the elaborate furniture of the room. The west and south sides of the room contain eleven panels, commencing within four feet of the floor, and extending eleven feet to the cornice at the ceiling. The panels, although of the same height, vary in width to suit the formation of the room and the divisions and openings made for business purposes. They are somewhat different in design from those in the ceiling, preserving, however, the same characteristics of blending the two-color woods into a harmonious whole. As a further ornament, and in order to mark distinctly the line between the panels, a heavy moulding of ebony extends around the outer edge of each compartment. Below these side panels, and running along the west and south walls of the room, is a base three feet in height. The panel form is still maintained with a bold moulding or rail to mark the division between the base and wainscoting above. The iron columns on Chestnut and Sixth Street fronts are also faced with panels of black walnut and butternut, to correspond with the finish in other portions of the room. At the north end of the office, against the west wall, and immediately in front of the counter, one form is still maintained, with a bold moulding or rail to indicate the division between the base and the panels above. The space, the size of a panel, has been filled with a mirror, eleven feet by five feet. This tends, by the reflection, to increase the apparent size of the room.

In the division of the office, care has been taken not

to mar the general effect of the work as a whole. Three divisions are made, the largest being twenty-three feet by forty, and known as the Publication Office proper. The second, for the Cashier, is thirteen feet by twenty-three; and the third, fitted up as the Private Office of Mr. Childs, is twelve feet by twenty-three feet. The form of the counter marks the separation between the Cashier and the Publication Office, there being an open-work screen above the counter two feet in height, filled in with plate-glass, the whole being similar to the elevations above the desks in banking establishments. The division between the Cashier's Room and the Private Office of the proprietor is made by means of an open framework of walnut, seven feet in height. Three arched openings, each five feet by four, pierce this partition. Two of these are filled with clear, fine, French plate-glass, in single sheets, the third containing a single plate, with the coat-of-arms of Philadelphia elaborately engraved, from B. H. Shoemaker's glass establishment. Resting on this partition is a large and elaborately carved Swiss clock with French movements.

The Private Office is subdivided into two rooms, the outer one being the reception or waiting-room, the partition between the two being little more than a frame for plate-glass, five feet by four feet, engraved with the coat-of-arms of Pennsylvania. The two doors, one leading from the inner room to the Cashier's Department, and the other to the Reception Room, are fitted with plate-glass, handsomely engraved around the edge, and containing in the centre the monogram "G. W. C."

The Private Office is furnished with the finest Wilton carpet, of a beautiful pattern in blue and gold; and all the furniture, of the Roman and Italian style, has been carved and made by Otton, to correspond with the design of the office. Mr. JOHN H. OTTON is one of the most accomplished architectural carvers in this country, and to him was intrusted all the elaborate carving throughout the building. In the execution of the work, he has achieved a signal triumph, and added still further to his reputation as an artist and mechanic. The doors leading to the Private Office contain glass in single sheets, six feet by two feet. A door leading to the hall on Sixth Street, as well as one opening into a Retiring Room at the south end of the apartment, is faced with mirrors six feet high and three feet wide. As none of the partitions extend in height more than seven feet, and these are all provided with the openings for glass, as we have described, the view of the business office is not in the least destroyed. The Retiring Room, referred to above, is an apartment at the south end of the room, extending under the stairway on the Sixth Street entrance to the building. It is ten feet by seven in dimensions, and has been fitted up to correspond with the main office, the sides and ceiling being oiled walnut and butternut-wood. Throughout this apartment every attention has been paid to the details required to make it what was desired in such a room. The carpet on this room is the same as that of the Private Office. Washstands of walnut, washbasin of pure white Italian marble, and the fixtures generally are of the most elaborate description. In the use of marble, the white Italian has been beautifully blended with the variegated Tennessee and the clouded California marble. The water-cooler in this room, by Struthers & Son, has been arranged in a manner different from the usual construction. The cooler is concealed, the silver spouts only appearing through a panel of white marble, around which runs a cornice of Tennessee marble. The panel has an arched top, in the centre of which is a keystone of California marble, with a monogram on its face. Provision has been made for the thorough ventilation of the room, and in every respect it is one of the most completely finished apartments in the building. All the modern conveniences, of the best material and most elaborate workmanship, have been introduced.

The labor and skill required in the construction of this magnificent Publication Office may be imagined when we state that there are nearly four thousand pieces of wood of various shapes and sizes in the wainscoting, all fitted and joined together with the nicety and exactness of the most beautiful article of cabinet-ware. Heavy walnut desks, of new design and construction, are provided for the Cashier and clerks.

The counter is another elaborate piece of work, by JOHN KILE, pattern-maker. It is of solid walnut and butternut-wood, the latter wood being used in the panels on the face. Heavy walnut brackets, carved in bold relief, ornament the front. The rear of the counter is provided with drawers and closets of walnut, and on the north end the "Post-Office" incident to a newspaper establishment is placed. In this connection we may state that a new feature in journalistic enterprise has been introduced into the new office, namely, a "Ladies' Department." A lady is in charge of the Post-Office, and attends to all the advertisements brought to the establishment by women. Against the west wall, and adjoining the Post-Office, a desk is provided for ladies preparing advertisements in the office. The Cashier's Department, Ladies' Department, and Post-Office are indicated by inscriptions on silver plates. To correspond with the counter, walnut seats, with carved legs and backs, have been constructed over the bulkheads, in order to accommodate customers with a resting-place in case of delay in the transaction of business. The centre panels of the backs of the benches or seats contain the monogram "G. W. C.," with "1836" on one side, and "1868" on the other. Prominent in the room are three handsome oiled walnut letter-boxes, of peculiar design, picked in with gold, and with silver plates engraved. All the cabinet-work, including sides and ceiling, has been prepared with oil and other materials known to the painter, until the whole has received what is called the "furniture finish," which, without the use of varnish, gives a gloss or polish similar to that put on modern cabinet-ware. This work was intrusted to BLUMNER & PALMER, the painters who took charge of the painting and cabinet-ware throughout the building.

The two fronts of the office, one on Chestnut and one on Sixth Street, give fifteen openings for doors and windows. There are six doors and nine windows. The windows are filled in with the best French plate-glass, in sheets twelve feet by five feet, while the doors are five feet in width and ten feet in height, with transom containing a plate of glass five feet by three feet.

The floor in front of the counter, as well as the floor of the Reception Room, is laid with black and white marble tile, in blocks twelve and six inches square. The contrast with the dark wood of the office is very fine. The floor in the rear of the counters is stained a dark color and polished. Heating apparatus, by the well-known firm of MORRIS, TASKER & Co., has been introduced, in the shape of coils of pipe inclosed in bronzed open-work iron stands, upon the top of which are white Italian marble slabs. The result of this arrangement is that, instead of being in any wise an obstruction, they are rather an ornament to the room. On one of these stands, situated in the northeast corner of the office, is a walnut stand of new design, containing portfolios intended for the daily file of the LEDGER, for inspection or use of customers who wish to refer to or cut the paper. Attached to it is a writing-desk. A second stand, in the south end of the room, contains on its top two handsome carved walnut writing-desks, with every convenience for customers to prepare their advertisements in the office. Behind the counter, there is a double desk, rising from a base of H form in plan, supported by four chimera legs boldly carved, the space beneath being arranged to receive sixteen business folios, four on each side of a Greek cross rotating so as to bring every book within the reach of the various clerks occupying the desk. In order to facilitate business, a "dumb-waiter" for "copy" is set in the side wall, and leads to the third and fifth stories, the former being the editorial and the latter the

Composing Room. Speaking-tubes also communicate with the various apartments, five hundred and sixty-eight feet of tube being used throughout the building for this purpose. To the tubes are attached Shannon's Patent Improved Indicator Mouthpieces.

The above description of the Publication Office gives but an imperfect idea at best of the magnificence, style, and finish of this room. It must be seen to be appreciated. This office is one of the most prominent features, not only in the building, but in Philadelphia.

THE PRESS ROOM.

Next to the Publication Office, the great feature of the establishment is the Press Room, which, in everything needed for the purpose of printing a newspaper, is without an equal in this or any other country. No expense has been spared to secure what was desired, and the result is alike creditable to the architect and those who were intrusted with the work. The basement appropriated to this department extends under the south wing of the building, and under the granite pavement of the street, at the rear of the Chestnut Street stores, and also under a portion of the Sixth Street sidewalk. This gives a room of an L shape, forty-six feet six inches wide, and running east and west one hundred and twenty-six feet, while the short arm of the L is eighty-nine feet by forty-two feet. Nine thousand one hundred and eighty-three square feet of space are thus obtained in which to place the presses, folding-machines, engines, boilers, steam-pumps, and all the appurtenances incident to the department. The height of the basement from floor to ceiling is twenty-three feet four inches. The ceiling is supported by fifteen immense columns, which are of wrought-iron of a peculiar construction, patented by SAMUEL J. REEVES, Esq., of the Phœnix Iron Company, in 1862, and now being generally introduced into first-class buildings of this character, and also into warehouses, depots, and bridges. These columns are seventeen inches in the diameter of the shaft, and twenty-one and a half inches counting from out to out of the filling pieces. The height, including cap and base, is twenty feet three inches; the weight per foot two hundred and eleven and one-third pounds; and the total weight of each column four thousand two hundred and eighty-nine pounds. The sectional area of shaft is fifty-five square inches; the required load seventy tons, which is equal to a little more than one and a quarter ton per inch. They were tested to a pressure of eighty tons, but at six tons per square inch their safe load is three hundred and thirty tons each. The fifteen columns will carry safely a load of five thousand tons, and would not be crippled under double that weight. These are the largest wrought-iron columns ever made, and were designed expressly for the LEDGER BUILDING. Their novelty consists in combining into a hollow shaft eight pieces of segment iron, having flanges on each edge their full length, and inserting between their flanges filling pieces five inches wide by three-quarters of an inch thick—the whole being riveted together and turned off true at each end for the cap and base. The effect produced by the projecting flanges and filling pieces is somewhat similar to that of large fluted columns, and is quite ornamental.

The Phœnix wrought-iron columns claim several important advantages over those of cast-iron. The pieces can all be rolled perfectly sound and true to section, and each piece can be examined in detail before it is used. The parts are all free from initial strains, and being rolled thin, the ratio of the diameter to the length can always be kept within the limit which will admit of a total applied pressure equal to the greatest elasticity of the iron in this, its best form. It is claimed to be not only safer and more reliable than the cast-iron column, but also much cheaper for equal service. Upon one series of these columns rests the northernmost brick wall of the projection under which this cellar is constructed. By this means the space be-

THE PUBLIC LEDGER BUILDING. 25

neath the granite slabs which cover the courtway or street is made part of the basement without the intervention of walls. Brick arches are thrown between the iron girders above, and these, as well as the side walls, are plastered and made in imitation of granite. The columns are also painted, with the small round projections which mark the bolts, bronzed. The whole finish is such as is rarely, if ever, found in an underground apartment. The "well-holes" referred to, and the vault-lights on the side street and on Sixth Street, give an abundance of ventilation and light to the immense room. Artificial light for night is

THE PRESS ROOM.

supplied through a large number of gas-burners distributed throughout the basement.

That portion of the basement extending under the Sixth Street pavement has a floor constructed midway between the ground and ceiling. This forms what may be called a long covered gallery for the accommodation of the carriers while waiting to receive their papers in the morning. In front of this, upon iron brackets extending into the cellar, and parallel with the Sixth Street front for twenty feet, is a gallery thrown open to the public. From this a good view of the operations of the presses can be obtained. In order to insure dryness in a cellar of the depth to which this has been carried, the ground has been levelled and paved with brick laid in cement. Over this three inches of asphaltum is laid, giving a floor almost as hard as stone and impervious to water. A well is in the northwest corner of the room. It contains a spring of water sufficient in quantity to supply a building double the size of the LEDGER BUILDING, independently of any connection with the street main. A beautifully finished "Woodward Steam Pump," capable of lifting seven thousand gallons of water per hour, is placed alongside of this well, ready for service in case of fire. It also forces the water to the tanks on the roof of the building, a distance of one hundred and twenty feet. From these tanks the building is supplied with water. The brick arches which form the ceiling of this room, as well as the general construction of the Press Room, were designed with especial reference to protection against fire.

The western end of the basement, thirty-three feet by thirty-five, is set apart as the Boiler Room, a brick partition, with openings for access between the two, separating it from the Press Room. Two of Harrison's boilers, each of fifty horse-power, are erected in this room, the work incident to the setting being of the most finished and substantial character. The coal-bins and ash-pits are easy of access to the engineer, and are arranged in such a manner as to insure the neat appearance of the Boiler Room at all times. Two of Brinton & Henderson's steam lifting-pumps are erected in this room, the office of one being to supply the boilers with water, the other to lift the waste-water from a well in the boiler room. Water is forced through ninety-five feet of pipe, and the pumps can throw three thousand gallons each per hour into the cisterns. The use to which the tanks are put will be referred to hereafter. There is a perfect labyrinth of pipes of all sizes leading from the boiler-room, all having some part in the general arrangement for heating the building or supplying it with water.

The engine, which is to drive the presses and furnish the motive power for the machinery in the job office, and other portions of the building, is located in the main room. Two solid slabs of granite, sixteen feet long, three and a half feet wide, and two feet thick, and weighing eight tons, form the bed upon which the engine securely rests. The engine has two cylinders, each of thirty-three horse-power, or a total of sixty-six horse-power. It is arranged upon the principle of a double engine, working at right angles. The engine was built by the Corliss Steam Engine Manufacturing Company of Providence, Rhode Island, and is a beautiful piece of machinery. It is a duplicate of one sent by the same Company to the Paris Exposition, and which received the first prize of a gold medal. All that science, skill, and attention could do has been combined in this engine.

Three of Hoe's Fast presses, with all the latest important improvements, and elegantly finished, will hereafter print the LEDGER. These machines will enable the paper to be run off much more rapidly than formerly. Each revolution of the type-carrying cylinder duplicates four pages four times; and the addition of a cutting machine to the press to divide the sheets as they pass from the cylinders, results in giving eight copies of the paper with every revolution of the type cylinder. With the increased facilities furnished by these improved presses, the already large and constantly increasing edition of the LEDGER can be ready for distribution to subscribers at a much earlier hour than formerly, and this will be the case should the circulation double its present number. As a further improvement, and in order to insure the prompt and early distribution of papers to carriers, and to relieve these gentlemen of the delay incident to preparing the sheets for subscribers, ten folding-machines have been provided. Nine of these have been constructed by CYRUS CHAMBERS, and one by BUCKLEY. All of these machines are of comparatively recent date, and are adapted to do expeditiously and properly the work heretofore intrusted to men. In a circulation as large as that of the LEDGER, an improvement of this character, shortening, as it does, the time required to manipulate each sheet, is no inconsiderable item.

Messrs. SELLERS & Co. furnished the shafting, pulleys, and gearing required for driving the powerful presses and machinery; and these, with the belting furnished by Messrs. SELLERS BROTHERS, were all specially manufactured for the purpose, and are of the most effective character.

In the minor details of the Press Room, as in every other department of the building, care has been observed to provide for the comfort of the employees, and those having business to transact in the basement. Wardrobes, washstands, and all the conveniences necessary for the accommodation of the workmen and carriers, have been considerately and liberally attended to.

THE COMPOSING ROOM.

The Composing Room will next attract attention, differing, as it does, from similar rooms in America or Europe. Instead of a dingy apartment of forbidding aspect, located in the least desirable part of the building, the Composing

THE PUBLIC LEDGER BUILDING. 29

Room of the LEDGER is one of the best-appointed and most thoroughly-finished portions of the edifice. The same attention to details that has marked the progress of the work on the entire structure from beginning to end is to be observed here. Nothing has been left undone that could in the least contribute to the comfort of the compositors and others, and enable them to perform expeditiously and properly their part in the publication of the LEDGER.

Situated in the fifth story, the addition of the Mansard roof gives a room of twenty-one feet from floor to ceiling, except under the central dome, where the height is thirty

THE COMPOSING ROOM.

feet. All that portion of the story, twenty-three feet wide, extending from Chestnut Street, along Sixth Street, a distance of one hundred and twenty-seven feet, is appropriated to the compositors. There are thus secured two thousand nine hundred and twenty-one square feet of space. The walls of the room are plastered and then painted in oil, the effect being to tone down the color, and remove the glare of the white plaster caused by the large number of windows on the several sides of the apartment. The southern wing is separated from the Composing Room by a partition, but it can, at any time, be added as part of the same room, should the necessities of the paper require it. Double the space now used would then be available. For the present the wing will be used as a store-room.

The northern end of the Composing Room has been railed off and neatly finished for the accommodation of the Proof Readers and Night Editors. In the remaining portions of the room, thirty-six stands for the compositors are erected. These stands have been located with reference to the use of the light supplied through the windows on Chestnut Street and the windows on Sixth Street, independently of the large glazed openings on either side of the Mansard roof. The arrangement of the stands is also made in such a manner as to avoid crowding the printers together, as is usual in many establishments, to the great inconvenience and annoyance of the men. Wash-room, clothes-rooms, and closets are provided as part of the Composing Room. The gas fixtures, instead of being suspended from the ceiling, come from the floor, and there is ample provision for an abundance of artificial light at each stand and throughout the room. In the fitting up of the room everything new has been introduced—new iron stands, new cases, new type, new proof press, new standing-galleys, new imposing stones, and new fixtures generally.

From the Composing Room access is had to the "look-out" on the roof of the building, a stairway leading to a small railed gallery, and thence to the roof.

THE STEREOTYPE FOUNDRY.

Adjoining the Composing Room, in the projection of what we have called the middle of the E plan of the building, is the Foundry for stereotyping the LEDGER. It is an apartment eighteen feet by thirty-five feet, lighted and ventilated by windows on the north and south sides. Great care has been taken in the construction of this room. In order to provide against fire, the floor is composed of iron girders, filled in with brick arches. Above these arches are placed several inches of gravel as the bed for a fine pressed-brick pavement. The walls are plastered and sprinkled in imitation of granite. At the west end of the room are the furnace and kettle for preparing the type-metal with which a cast of the LEDGER is taken every night for use on the presses. The furnace and kettle are of new and improved construction. All the fixtures, including the moulds, steam-chest, cutting-machines, bed-plates, &c., are new and of the best material, with the latest improvements. At the end of the passage-way, running at right angles with the foundry, are the hoisting apparatus and the well-hole communicating with the Press Room below, and by means of which the stereotype plates are transferred from the Foundry to the pressmen to be used in printing the LEDGER.

EDITORIAL ROOMS.

The third story, twenty-three feet on Chestnut Street and sixty-five feet on Sixth, is appropriated to the editorial rooms. Those who are familiar with the interior of newspaper establishments, and accustomed to visit rooms usually assigned to the literary staff, will be astonished to find in the new LEDGER building, instead of contracted and awkwardly arranged quarters, a suite of magnificently frescoed apartments, fitted up in drawing-room style.

There are four rooms designed to accommodate the Editors and Reporters. One room, at the corner of Sixth and Chestnut, is twenty-three by thirty feet, and is known as the Library, and is occupied principally by the managing Editor. The walls and ceiling are beautifully frescoed in panels, the prevailing color being a light green, with mouldings, cornice, and centre-piece of imitation walnut, with scroll-work running through, picked in with red and decorated with the tints necessary to mark the lines in the artist's design. All the wood-work of the windows and doors is walnut, and the chandeliers and gas fixtures are bronzed. The furniture and appointments of this room are of the most elaborate workmanship, and prepared expressly for the purpose, by MOORE & CAMPION, from original designs. A rich crimson and gold Wilton carpet covers the floor, and the furniture consists of neatly framed photographs, paintings, &c., also lounges, mirrors, carved secretary, chairs, and octagon table, all of oiled walnut. Heating pipe, inclosed in an ornamental framework of iron, with marble top, has been introduced into this and the adjoining rooms. Handsome shades at the windows complete the furnishing of the Library. The adjoining rooms, three in number, communicate one with another and with the Library, and all open on to a wide hall running north and south from the stairway leading to the third story. Each of these rooms is frescoed with panels of a light cream color, with ornamental borders and centre-pieces. The work is grained to imitate oak, and the furniture is made to correspond. Book-cases, newspaper files, tables and secretaries, desks, wardrobes, lounges, and chairs are provided for those who occupy these rooms. The one adjoining the Library is the Editorial Room proper; the next is assigned to the Reporters; and the third is the Financial Editor's department. The fresco work and painting were executed by Blumner & Palmer.

THE JOB PRINTING OFFICE.

The Job Office is on the third floor, and occupies a space embraced within the new additions to the building. It is in the form of a letter F, the portion on Sixth Street being seventy-eight feet by twenty-three, while the extension westward in the southern wing is thirty-six feet by a hundred and sixteen feet. The middle projection gives eighteen feet by thirty-five additional. The formation of the room furnishes five thousand seven hundred and seventy-two square feet of space. As this room contains a large amount of machinery, including the presses for job work, it was necessary to secure a firm foundation, and at the same time provide against annoyances to tenants in the offices below consequent upon the jar and rumble of running machinery. In order to accomplish what was desired, heavy iron girders form the floor of this portion of the third story. Above these is the ordinary arrangement of joists. The wooden girders are securely braced and bolted, and filled in with boards, upon which four inches of tan is placed. Over the tan the flooring boards are framed together. This gives strength and stability to the floor, and the use of tan deadens the sound and will prevent any disturbance of those occupying the story below by reason of noise. To provide a firm backing for the shafting in this room, the ceiling, instead of being plastered, is covered with flooring boards, painted white. A neat walnut counter, for business purposes, and an office, railed off for the superintendent of the Job Office, are in the north end of the room. In view of the large and constantly increasing demands upon the Job Office, the presses, fixtures, and machinery provided for the work are of the best material and neatest finish, and combine all the latest improvements. Hoe's, Adams', and Gordon's presses have been provided in numbers calculated to execute with dispatch all orders intrusted to this department.

The numerous windows on the front, and rear, and sides give abundance of light and ventilation to the rooms, and make it one of the best and most conveniently arranged Job Offices in any printing establishment in Philadelphia or elsewhere.

THE BOOK PUBLICATION OFFICE.

The office for the transaction of the business connected with the book publications of Mr. Childs is on the second story, and located in the middle projection of the building. It is neatly fitted up with all that is necessary for the prompt and systematic attention to this department of the establishment.

We have thus far described only that portion of this immense building used for purposes connected with the printing of the LEDGER, and the publication of the LITERARY GAZETTE AND PUBLISHERS' CIRCULAR and the LAW WORKS issued by Mr. Childs. Attached to all these apartments are water-closets, arranged with all the modern conveniences. From first to last, inside and out, nothing has been omitted and nothing has been slighted. On the contrary, all that artistic taste and mechanical skill could supply, aided by a liberal outlay of money, has been taken advantage of to secure a building not only ornamental and imposing when viewed from the exterior, but which should at the same time contain within its walls machines, machinery, apparatus, fixtures, and furniture of the best workmanship, finest finish, and most durable character.

Having thus disposed of the apartments used by the LEDGER Establishment, it is our purpose next to refer to the uses to which the remainder of the building has been put.

THE STORES.

There are three stores, two on Chestnut Street, and one on Sixth. In the original construction of the building, there were four stores on Chestnut Street. In the new plan, one of them has been taken for the Publication Office; a second has been left the original width, but extended in depth, while the remaining two have been thrown into one, making a store of good proportions. This large store was fitted up by Mr. Childs expressly for A. T. STEWART & Co., the well-known and extensive New York drygoods merchants. It is thirty-six feet front, extending back on the first floor a distance of one hundred and eleven feet, to the street or courtway leading into George's Court, and thence to Sansom Street. Fluted iron columns fourteen inches in diameter, with attic base and Corinthian cap, have been substituted for the wall that formerly divided this store into two. This arrangement is continued throughout the building occupied by Mr. Stewart, and gives him a large open space on each floor for the storage of goods and the transaction of business. At right angles with the rear of the store is a large passage eighteen feet wide, extending into Sixth Street, giving an outlet in that direction, as well as to the rear before mentioned.

The first story of the store is fifteen feet ten inches from floor to ceiling, the second thirteen feet, the third, fourth, and fifth each ten feet. The ceiling of the room on the first floor is finished in panels of wood instead of plaster. This, as well as all the woodwork inside the stores, is painted white, and while there is nothing in the decorations that may be called grand, there are few stores in Philadelphia provided with better facilities for the transaction of business. The stairways inside this and the adjoining store have heavy walnut railing extending from the first to the fifth story. Improved hoisting apparatus, by WILLIAM SELLERS & Co., is also introduced into both stores. Bronzed two-light chandeliers extend throughout the building. The front of the store on Chestnut Street contains six openings, four of which are windows with fine French plate glass in single sheets, similar to those in the Publication Office. Under Mr. Stewart's store there are a well-lighted basement and a sub-cellar, running the whole length of the building.

The westernmost store is occupied by CADBURY, RHOADS & THOMAS, drygoods commission merchants. Its construction is similar to the store just described, except that it is twenty-six feet front, instead of thirty-six feet, and has no outlet on Sixth Street. It is finished the same as that occupied by Mr. Stewart. The tenants occupy the five stories.

On Sixth Street, the store which adjoins the Publication Office on the south is occupied by B. C. WORTHINGTON, tobacconist. His store is eighteen feet front by twenty-three feet in depth, and is fitted with the French glass on the front, to correspond with that on other portions of the building.

THE OFFICES.

Next come the offices on the first and second floors of the extension on Sixth Street, and in the southern projection at right angles with Sixth Street, and also on the second floor immediately over the Publication Office. The latter room is of the same size as the Publication Office, and is occupied by BRADSTREET'S Improved Commercial Agency. It is an office well suited to the purpose, and the tenants have fitted it up in handsome style, with walnut fixtures, desks, and furniture. Independently of this room there are thirty-one offices—thirteen on the first floor, and eighteen on the second. On the first floor three of the offices front on Sixth Street, and are supplied with French plate glass. In the second story, six offices front on Sixth Street. The remainder of the rooms are distributed along the southern projection. A passage-way, six feet wide, runs east and west through the middle of the wing, and the offices are situated on either side of it—those to the north receiving light through windows in the rear cartway, and those on the south being supplied by means of the "well-holes" before referred to. The well-holes also furnish light to the hall. A second hall runs along the rear of the offices fronting on Sixth Street. The entire range of offices on both floors, except the three on the first floor front, and those located with reference to the well-holes, communicate with one another, and can, therefore, be rented singly or in suites. The rooms are nearly of the same size, averaging fifteen feet by sixteen feet in dimensions, and thirteen feet from floor to ceiling. All are well ventilated and lighted, and steam-pipes, supplied from the LEDGER boilers, will furnish the heat in the winter. Neat gas fixtures have been introduced into all the offices. Two of the offices on the second floor, fronting on Sixth Street, are occupied by Mr. DOBBINS, the builder, who has fitted them up in good taste, having had the ceilings and walls frescoed in colors similar to the Editorial Rooms.

In the fourth story, E. TRACY & Co., extensive watch-case-makers, occupy the southern projection, a room thirty-six feet by a hundred and sixteen feet. The front part on Sixth Street has been arranged as a counting-room, neatly furnished, while the rear is filled with the benches and fine machinery incident to the business. The ceiling of this room has been constructed of planed boards instead of plaster, in view of the shafting used. Steam-power is obtained from the LEDGER engines.

On the same floor, at right angles with Tracy's establishment, is a room nineteen feet by fifty-one feet, fronting on Sixth Street, occupied by VAN INGEN & SNYDER, wood engravers; and another room, on the corner of Sixth and Chestnut Streets, of the same size as the one occupied for the Commercial Agency. There is still another room in the projection, the same size as the Foundry above.

This completes the description of the building, and in this connection nothing remains but to indicate the means of

ACCESS TO THE ROOMS.

The main stairway leading to the upper portion of the building is on Sixth Street, through a hall nine feet wide, adjoining the southern end of the Publication Office. This stairway is imposing and of easy ascent, a platform being arranged midway in each story. The stairway leads to the fourth story, a closed stairway extending from thence to the Composing Room. A handsome walnut rail runs the entire flight, with a heavy walnut cap, while the corresponding elevation against the wall of the stairway is faced with walnut and butternut-wood in alternate slips, all neatly finished and oiled.

From the fourth to the fifth story, in addition to the closed stairway forming the continuation of the main stairs, there is one of similar construction at the north side of Tracy's establishment. At the southern end of the Sixth Street front there is another open stairway, leading to the second story, and intended for the use of those occupying the offices or having business with the tenants of these rooms. It is furnished with a handsome walnut rail, similar to the one attached to the main stairway. In the rear, at the western end of the southern projection, there is also a closed stairway leading from the first floor to the upper portion of the building. Hatchways, with hoisting apparatus, are also located in this portion of the building. Access is had to the Press Room from two stairways on Sixth Street, and a private one leading from the hall adjoining the Publication Office.

THE WATER SUPPLY

In a building of the magnitude and construction of the LEDGER establishment, great care and skill were required in the arranging of the water supply to the various stories and departments. The work, together with the arrangement of the fixtures for the water-closets, was intrusted to JOSEPH W. FORSYTH, plumber. He has executed the work in a satisfactory manner. Four thousand five hundred feet of pipe have been used to convey water from the tanks at the top of the building to the thirty-four water-closets and other portions of the edifice where it is needed. Pipe has also been distributed with reference to protection against fire, and at every available spot a plug, with attachments for hose, has been located. Hose is placed at each story, within easy reach in case of fire; a total of three hundred and fifty feet is used for this purpose. The two tanks used to collect the water are of a capacity of three thousand gallons each. All the pipe, except that supplying the first story, leads from these tanks, thus securing at all times a uniform supply and pressure in every part of the building.

GENERAL DETAILS.

Combining stability and graceful architectural lines, the building, as a whole, may be aptly termed a huge crystal palace, uniting with the solidity of a pile of brown stone all the light and delicate tracery of an edifice of glass. It contains sixty-four thousand eight hundred and twelve square feet of space, and is lighted by three hundred and fifty-four windows, with a total of two thousand eight hundred and twenty-four panes of glass, independently of the sheet glass in the first-story fronts on Sixth and Chestnut Streets. About five hundred thousand pounds of iron, wrought and cast, supplied by the PHŒNIX IRON COMPANY, JOHN LANDELL, and SHEPPARD, MORTON & LEECH, have been used in the construction of the building. Some twenty thousand feet of tin (exclusive of slating) have been used to cover the flat portion of the roofs alone. Much of this work, where joining with stone and iron projections, though of a most intricate character, has been executed by CHARLES DONAGHY in an excellent manner. The smith-work was done by MATSINGER BROS., whose contract embraced all the stays, braces, eyes, anchors, camber-rods, skylight sash and grating, together with the fire-proofs and awning-frames, which have all been completed in that substantial and tasteful manner which marks the work of this noted firm. Six thousand five hundred feet of pipe have been used to distribute gas to the various rooms in the building. The work was done by GODFREY KROUSE, the fixtures being supplied by MISKEY, MERRILL & THACKARA. Fifteen thousand three hundred and thirty-nine feet of tube were used in the heating-pipes and coils required to distribute warmth throughout the building. This portion of the contract was awarded to MORRIS, TASKER & Co., who took a great deal of pains to make their work thorough and satisfactory. COMBER & Co. had charge of the granite-work, which is finished in the most substantial manner throughout. Mr. R. J. DOBBINS, the builder, who was ably seconded by his brother, MURREL DOBBINS, brick-layer, and GEORGE GLAYSTINE, carpenter, brought the entire work to a successful termination, and the splendid pile will long remain a monument of his skill, an ornament to the city, and an evidence of the public spirit and liberality of the projector and owner.

Some idea of the size of the structure may be gathered when it is understood that to pass around the several apartments above the pavement will involve a journey of one thousand seven hundred and ninety-eight yards, or a trifle over a mile, and that upwards of forty thousand days' work was performed on the building.

PUBLIC LEDGER BUILDING.

Southwest corner of 6th and Chestnut Streets.

Commenced May, 1866. Completed June, 1867.

Proprietor.
GEORGE W. CHILDS.

General Manager. Superintendent of Press Room.
WM. V. McKEAN. **W. L. DRANE.**

Architect. Assistant Architect.
J. McARTHUR, Jr. **GEORGE SUMMERS.**

General Contractor and Builder.
RICHARD J. DOBBINS.

Contractors for Brown Stone and Marble.
STRUTHERS & SON.

Sculptor.
J. A. BAILLY.

Sub-Contractors and Superintendents.

Excavations	McNichols & Bro.
Granite Work	Comber & Co.
Cast Iron	John Landell.
" "	Sheppard, Morton & Leech.
Rolled Iron	Phœnix Iron Co.
Smith Work	Matsinger Bros.
Superintendent Carpenters	George Glaystine.
" Masons and Brickwork	Murrel Dobbins.
" Plastering	George James.
Painting	Blumner & Palmer.
Tinwork	Charles Donaghy.
Slating	Jason Lewis & Co.
Plumbing	J. W. Forsyth.
Gas Fixtures and Bronzes	Miskey, Merrill & Thackara.
Gas Fitting	Godfrey Krouse.
Hardware	Field & Hardie.
"	J. D. Shannon.
Iron Stairs, &c.	Robert Wood & Co.
Iron Railing	White & Devinney.
Carved Furniture	John H. Otton.
" "	Moore & Campion.
Counter Work	John Kile.
Stairs and Walnut Railing	Grubb & Hines.
Ornamental and French Glass	B. H. Shoemaker.
Steam Heating	Morris, Tasker & Co.
Boilers	Joseph Harrison, Jr.
Steam Hoists, Shafting, &c.	Wm. Sellers & Co.
Wire Screens	Walker & Sons.
Lightning Rods and Vanes	J. D. Rice.

Time Clerk for Mechanics and Laborers.
WM. McARTHUR.

Opening

OF THE

New Ledger Building.

OPENING OF THE NEW LEDGER BUILDING.

On Thursday, the 20th of June, 1867, the NEW LEDGER BUILDING was formally opened, the event being marked by a gathering of newspaper men from all parts of the country, who were invited to be present to assist at the inaugural ceremonies. During Wednesday the numerous workmen were busily engaged in giving the finishing touches to the edifice, and preparing it for the inspection of visitors. Success attended their efforts, and, with the exception of a few trifling details, the building presented a finished appearance. At 12 o'clock precisely the magnificent flags presented by the Messrs. Horstmann were thrown to the breeze, the National, State, and City colors being displayed from the flagstaffs. At 3 o'clock the guests began to arrive at the building, and in a short time there was a brilliant gathering of representative men. The literary, mechanical, and mercantile world, together with clergymen of the different denominations, poets and authors, judges and lawyers, physicians, architects, artists, writers and publishers, were represented. Military and naval men, as well as civilians, were present, and never before in the history of Philadelphia was there ever seen a more distinguished gathering of gentlemen who had made their mark in the world.

A pleasant hour was spent in examining the building, after which the company assembled in the large Composing Room in the fifth story.

About 4 o'clock the assemblage was called to order by Judge F. C. BREWSTER, who said:—

GENTLEMEN: You will please come to order. The agreeable duty has been assigned me of requesting the Hon. CHARLES GILPIN, formerly Mayor of this city, now District Attorney of the United States, and well known to all of us, to be kind enough to take the chair upon this occasion.

REMARKS OF MR. GILPIN.

Mr. Gilpin came forward, and, when the applause with which he was received had partially subsided, spoke as follows:—

GENTLEMEN: I acknowledge the honor of the call to the chair upon this occasion, and while I do so I may be permitted to say that it is perhaps attributable in part to the relations which I have held, as chief magistrate of this city, with the Philadelphians who are here present, and to the knowledge which our stranger friends who are with us have of me arising out of that relation.

But, perhaps, there is another reason why the call may not be considered entirely inappropriate. I have long known and intimately known the founders of the LEDGER, and I have always had most pleasant relations with its present proprietor, Mr. Childs. I have known the LEDGER throughout its whole life, "egg and bird;" and I recollect when Mr. Swain, my old friend, and I used to be about in the "wee sma' hours" of the morning to get the news from it before the public were awake. It was "a penny-wise" but never "a pound-foolish" paper [applause]; and the "two-penny" policy which has been adopted by the successor of Mr. Swain, though a question of some doubt at the time, together with other changes that he made in it, has convinced the public and some of those who did not altogether agree with him in opinion, that he was as wise, and in some things a little wiser, than his predecessor. That the prosperity which has arisen from that source will continue with him is, I know, the ardent hope of all present. [Great applause.]

The LEDGER—you are all as well acquainted with it as I am—what need I say of it? It has been a peculiar paper. It is the only paper, perhaps, in the United States that without great profession has started upon and adhered to a sound moral basis and a moderate, conservative course; I mean, of the papers that have been self-sustaining. There are other papers that have started with great proclamations of what they proposed to accomplish in the maintenance of morals and religion, yet none of them have stood up more determinedly than the LEDGER for the vindication of correct principles; comparatively speaking, they have proved failures. The LEDGER has been temperate, wise, discreet; never flattering any one on account of his position, and never assailing any one because he happened to be a poor devil of a fellow whom it was easy to kick. It has been temperate in those things, and that has been the foundation of its success.

I knew the original proprietors well. I had great respect for them, and great confidence in their common sense and in their ability. I know the present proprietor very well, and I think he is a most able and worthy successor, and from what we see here to-day, and from what has occurred in the management of the paper, we may safely predict that he will meet a proper reward for the enterprise which he has exhibited. It is not a mere question of the LEDGER: it is a question of Philadelphia and the LEDGER [applause], because these things go hand in hand, with equal pace. If Philadelphia was not ready and willing to receive the LEDGER as it is published, and to acknowledge the enterprise which attends it as it is manifested by its proprietor, Philadelphia would not be what it has always been; but while this building is an indication of the prosperity of the establishment, it is an indication, too, of the prosperity and progress of the city of Philadelphia. [Applause.] From being once a local paper, the LEDGER has now become a standard paper, a national paper. It is known and received and read all over the country; it is an institution of the city of Philadelphia; it is a type of our progress, a type of our prosperity; and I believe that our city is moving on rapidly, and that with it the LEDGER and all interested in it will continue to prosper. [Long-continued applause.]

In conclusion, permit me to say, I believe we have with us a gentleman who has contributed much to the elevation of this great structure. I refer to Mr. McArthur. The gentlemen present will be glad to see him, and to hear from him too.

REMARKS OF MR. JOHN McARTHUR, Jr., ARCHITECT.

Mr. JOHN McARTHUR, JR., the Architect of the building, in response to the numerous calls made upon him, then stepped forward and said:—

MR. CHAIRMAN AND GENTLEMEN: As Architect for Mr. Childs, I would respond to Mr. Gilpin by remarking, that perhaps no professor of the arts has felt, in the past, more intensely than the Architect, the want of cultivated and liberal minds to appreciate and execute his immaterial creations; nor are such wants, even in these days of public progress and enterprise, yet wholly unknown. Although, as a Philadelphian, I am proud of the increasing taste and liberality of her citizens, as evidenced in the substantial and elegant buildings, both public and private, which now adorn her streets, I cannot but feel increased pleasure at the financial courage and princely liberality of Mr. George W. Childs, to whom we this day owe the NEW LEDGER BUILDING. But little more than twelve months ago, most of the space on which we stand was occupied by time-worn and dilapidated structures, which, outliving their time, have been swept down by relentless progress, and from whose very graves has sprung this colossal pile. Early in the spring of 1866, through the good offices of a large-hearted friend (the late Dr. Jayne), I was commissioned by Mr. Childs to design a suitable building in which

OPENING.

to accommodate the PUBLIC LEDGER, whose extraordinary increasing business demanded facilities commensurate with its immense circulation and influence. The present site being purchased, I was directed to proceed with the drawings, untrammelled by that too common stumbling-block of the architect, limited expenditure. Plans and specifications were soon prepared and submitted to competent builders for proposals. With many doubts and fears lest the unsettled condition and greatly increased cost of labor and materials should prevent the execution of the design, I waited most anxiously the opening of the bids; and although the lowest of them greatly exceeded my extreme estimates, Mr. Childs at once decided to proceed with the work, awarding to Mr. R. J. Dobbins the general contract, and to Mr. Struthers all the stone fronts. Such promptness in the face of so large a proposed expenditure is rare, more particularly when it was evident to both the owner and myself that the business of the LEDGER could as readily be accommodated in a plain, substantial building, at a saving in cost of not less than one hundred thousand dollars. To the contractors, Mr. Dobbins and Mr. Struthers, together with the able mechanics and others furnishing labor or materials, much praise is due, they all having done their best to sustain the well-merited character for excellence so universally accorded to Philadelphia workmen.

For such information as was necessary to a proper arrangement of apartments and apparatus for the efficient working of this great publishing house, I and my assistant, Mr. George Summers, are almost wholly indebted to the far-seeing and comprehensive views of Mr. Childs, the proprietor, and to Mr. McKean, the general manager, and Mr. Drane, the mechanical superintendent of the PUBLIC LEDGER; our duty being to give strength and stability to their numerous suggestions and requirements, and adapt the whole to architectural forms. The success or failure of our efforts is before you, subject to your inspection and criticism. And here let me say, in closing, that experience and observation in the practice of my profession have taught me to believe that none of the arts so impresses the mind through the eye as Architecture; and just in proportion as its purity is fostered and esteemed by any people will they be found refined and cultivated. How appropriate, then, and consistent, that the PUBLIC LEDGER, daily addressing more than three hundred thousand readers and hearers, should also commend itself to an appreciating public by a spacious and tasteful edifice, a lasting evidence of its stability and power.

Mr. R. J. DOBBINS, the Builder, was then called upon. By request of Mr. Dobbins, the Hon. DANIEL M. FOX responded to the call.

REMARKS OF HON. DANIEL M. FOX.

He said that, although one of our most energetic and successful builders, his friend was an exceedingly modest man. To make a speech under circumstances such as the present was for him, as he said, one of the most embarrassing duties that could be assigned him. That gentleman's task in the fulfilment of his portion of the contract had been to him an exceedingly anxious and protracted one, and he had devoted many days and even nights to thought and labor in his anxiety and determination to make the building not only a credit to himself, but a complete realization of the idea of its public-spirited owner—in a word, to make it an important addition to the ornamental architecture of the city. Having received the assurance of Mr. Childs that his work had given full satisfaction, Mr. Dobbins wished to make it known that, in a very material degree, his success was due to the kind forbearance and liberal spirit which had ever distinguished that gentleman in their intercourse from the beginning to the end of the great work, and he desired to express his thanks to Mr. Childs thus publicly. [Applause.]

REMARKS OF MR. WM. V. McKEAN.

Wm. V. McKean, Esq., of the Ledger, being called upon, came forward and said:—

Gentlemen: We have just heard from one modest man, and I am here to speak for another—and that other is Mr. Childs. [Applause.] I know that he has experienced a great deal of anxiety about this building during the last eighteen months; but I feel very free to say, that rather than get up and make a speech here for himself, he would undergo all that anxiety for the next eighteen months.

Now, I am certainly not warranted in speaking at any length to an audience scattered about as this one is, and from a platform no higher than the one on which I stand, and I will detain you perhaps but five or ten minutes; for you are due at five o'clock at the Continental. You will please to bear in mind, gentlemen, in construing all that I may say, that I am sufficiently identified with this establishment to know what I am talking about, and that, at the same time, I am sufficiently disconnected from Mr. Childs to be able to speak in praise of him without any risk of self-laudation. Therefore, if I praise him, you will please bear in mind my explanation. The object sought to be accomplished in the erection of this magnificent structure in which we are assembled to-day, was—first, to build a printing-office that would be as thoroughly adapted to the purpose, and as convenient as any printing-office could be made; second, to make that printing-office a comfortable, cheerful, and wholesome place for workmen to do their work in—a very important desideratum. The third consideration (growing from and not interfering with the other two) was to make this convenient, comfortable, and wholesome printing-office an ornament to the city of Philadelphia. [Applause.]

Now, gentlemen, you have been over this building, and you are able to judge (even those of you who are not printers) whether, in the first place, it is likely to make a convenient printing-office. You who have seen that light and airy, dry and well-ventilated press-room, although it is twenty feet below the pavement (and which, in printing-offices ordinarily, is a dark, damp, unwholesome well to work in), and you who stand now beneath this lofty ceiling, where a hundred gas-lights will be burning every night, and where there are space and ventilation provided for carrying off the devitalized air, the air whose oxygen has been consumed, and that would otherwise poison and ultimately destroy the lungs of the workmen—you, too, who have seen the luxurious apartments which those of us who are otherwise occupied are to inhabit—you may be able to say whether the office is a convenient place, and whether its arrangements are such as will be likely to conduce to the sanitary good of the men who are to work within the building. And those of you who have looked at it from without, may be able to answer, as well as Mr. Childs or I, or anybody could do, whether this magnificent structure which has arisen here at Sixth and Chestnut Streets, is an ornament to the city of Philadelphia. [Applause.] And when you have considered these points, gentlemen, you will be able to answer whether the three great objects aimed at by Mr. Childs in the plan and arrangement of the building have been successfully achieved or not. [Prolonged applause.]

This brings me naturally and logically to the point where I may properly speak of the gentlemen who have had this matter in charge: of Mr. McArthur, the architect, whose genius and experience have been all the time operating; of Mr. Dobbins, the builder, whose skill as an artisan has all the time been operating; of his brother whom I see here before me; of the various sub-contractors who are named in the papers of this day—that to them altogether, to their heads and hands, and to all the active energies they have displayed, we owe the execution of the admirable plans and designs of Mr. Childs for this magnificent building. I wish they had spoken more for themselves, but I will say their work is done well throughout, from the first drawings of the architect to the last stone that was put upon the building.

Now, gentlemen, there are some of you who perhaps have heard something about the cost of this building. I am not going to say what the aggregate cost is, but I will mention a few things connected with it. In the putting up of this building several hundred thousand dollars have gone out into circulation among the stone-masons, the bricklayers, the brickmakers, the carpenters, the plasterers, the painters, the blacksmiths, the locksmiths, the gas-fitters, the steam-fitters, the carvers, the cabinet-makers, and the machinists and other workmen of this community. In furnishing the building with machinery to do its work, somewhere in the neighborhood of one hundred thousand dollars more have gone into the foundries, the machine shops, and other workshops of this city; so that you will perceive something has been accomplished in keeping the circulating medium in action in that way, instead of locking it up in a grand investment of an inactive kind. It is in just that sort of thing that Mr. Childs, who has been referred to here as a modest man, takes delight; and I say it is a characteristic for which any man ought to be honored: that he should prefer to invest in a way in which all these agencies of industry, all these workshops, are put in vigorous action.

I have said enough as to the mere cost of the thing, and I think, from the look of the clock, I ought to be coming to a close. There is a great deal else that might be said, but I will only detain you now to say this: that you, gentlemen, who are here and have seen this beautiful building, and heard something of what it has cost, must not go away with the impression that the million or more dollars that are invested in the business have been the profits of the LEDGER within a year or so. [Laughter.] I feel bound to warn you all not to go to setting up newspapers with any idea of acquiring suddenly such an income as that out of the business. [Renewed laughter.] A great amount of money has been spent here which did not come out of the profits of the LEDGER at all.

Mr. Chairman: I believe I have done all now I ought to do except to thank Mr. McArthur, Mr. R. J. Dobbins, and all the sub-contractors engaged in this work, and to say in behalf of Mr. Childs, that this building, as far as their work is completed, is accepted from their hands with very great satisfaction.

Judge BREWSTER said: Mr. Chairman, I move that we adjourn to the Continental Hotel.

Adjourned.

Banquet at the Continental Hotel.

BANQUET AT THE CONTINENTAL HOTEL.

At the close of the ceremonies at the building, the company adjourned to the Continental Hotel, where a magnificent banquet had been prepared for the entertainment of the distinguished guests. In preparing for this banquet, J. E. Kingsley & Co., the proprietors of the Continental, had a *carte blanche*, and in execution of the order intrusted to them, they succeeded in preparing an entertainment the like of which had never been seen in Philadelphia. The splendid large banqueting room of the Continental was filled with tables spread for the guests. A table ran along the entire length of the room, with ten others at right angles with it, and these were handsomely decorated with all that confectionery art and artistic taste could furnish, while all the table furniture, of silver and French china, was of the brightest and newest patterns. The rarest and choicest flowers and tasteful pyramids were interspersed with the elaborate constructions of confectionery. On the main table a representation of the old hand-press contrasted with Hoe's Last-Fast; and perhaps the most striking figure was a representation of the NEW LEDGER BUILDING, constructed of a material known only to the chief caterer; and it was a capital representation of the building.

The decorations of the room were of a character to correspond with the tables and their contents. The American flag was draped around the room, with a centre-piece over the presiding officer's chair. This centre-piece was an arrangement of the national colors around the coat-of-arms of the State, the whole forming a tableau of great beauty.

The Germania Orchestra was in attendance, and throughout the evening discoursed most excellent music. The Mænnerchor Society was also present, and, during the pauses in the speeches, gave some of their best songs and choruses in German and English. The Star-Spangled Banner was especially noticed.

It is scarcely possible fully to describe the splendor of the spectacle presented in the vast saloon, when the thronging guests had seated themselves around the tables. We are dealing not in hyperbole, but with facts, when we say, that the brilliancy of the scene had never before been surpassed or equalled in our country. All the resources of art, taste, skill, and unbounded liberality were invoked to lend grace to the occasion; and those who witnessed it will ever recall it as a great event in their lives. Brave men, and wise men—rulers of armies, cities, and States—legislators and lawyers, teachers of religion and judges of courts, authors and journalists, merchants and bankers, gathered from various States of the Union, were there found side by side, joining in willing homage to the power of the Press, and celebrating an illustrious triumph of its enterprise. Thus the sight presented was rendered no less suggestive to the thought than impressive to the sense of the beholder.

About five hundred guests were seated at the tables among whom were representatives of the press of the whole country, forming one grand family, in which all questions of politics were sunk in the universal recognition of the dignity of the profession to which they belonged. Mayor McMichael presided, and, celebrated as he is for tact and genial humor in giving happy direction to all the proceedings at social and festive meetings, it was a subject of universal remark that his felicitous and admirable management on this occasion could not have been surpassed.

The pleasures of the evening were enjoyed by a number of ladies, as well as the distinguished body of representative men already referred to. The ladies were assembled in an adjoining parlor, where a sumptuous dinner had been set by Mr. Kingsley, and after it was over, they adjourned to the large dining-hall, and spent the remainder of the evening in listening to the admirable speaking that marked the occasion. This was a pleasant and unique feature of the PUBLIC LEDGER celebration.

The ceremonies of the evening were opened by BISHOP SIMPSON, who invoked the Divine blessing in the following

PRAYER.

ALMIGHTY FATHER! we adore thee as the Creator of all worlds, the bountiful Giver of every good and perfect gift. All light emanates from thee; thou art the source of wisdom and of knowledge! We praise thee for the multitude of thy mercies; for thy thoughts of love and compassion to the human family; for the inspirations which purify and elevate our race! We confess our sins, and implore forgiveness through our blessed Redeemer. We pray for the gift of the Holy Spirit, that in all our ways we may hereafter please thee.

Assembled as we are at this hour, we bless thee for the art of printing, for the diffusion of literature, and for all the holy influences which flow thence upon society. We implore thy richest benedictions upon thy servant at whose invitation we have convened, and by whose hands these tables have been furnished. Long may he live to enjoy the smiles of thy countenance, and to do good among men. Bless all who have assembled here from different parts of our land. May all those who are connected with the press in its various offices be teachers of wisdom, and may they all be taught of God. May their influence ever be powerful in removing evil, and in elevating society towards its high perfection. May we all so eat and drink, so live and labor, that we shall fulfil our mission on earth, and finally meet in heaven, for Christ's sake. Amen!

The numerous and delicious courses of the banquet occupied several hours, which rapidly passed away during an incessant flow of sallies of wit and agreeable and genial conversation. After the disposition of the feast, the further proceedings of the evening were inaugurated by the eloquent and impressive delivery of the following

ADDRESS OF MAYOR McMICHAEL.

GENTLEMEN: Mr. Childs has asked me to occupy, this evening, the place which, as our host, under ordinary circumstances, he would be expected to fill. I have acceded to this request very cheerfully, not only because it always gives me pleasure to oblige Mr. Childs, but, also, because it seems to me proper that somebody other than himself should preside. The motives which have brought us together are peculiar. We are the guests of Mr. Childs [applause]—bidden by him to this most generous and sumptuous feast; but at the same time we have assembled not merely, nor even so much, that he may do honor to us, as that we may do honor to him [great applause], or rather to the event it is his object to commemorate. It is well, therefore, that he should be relieved from the embarrassments which this dual, and in some respects incongruous, position might involve; and there are obvious reasons, both official and professional, why I should take his seat. In doing so, of course I commit myself to the double duty of speaking for him and for you. [Applause.]

First, then, gentlemen, in behalf of Mr. Childs, let me say that he rejoices at your presence. For months past he has looked to the completion of the NEW LEDGER BUILDING as a crowning act in his career. No wonder, therefore, that he desired to consummate its dedication to his future uses by suitable ceremonies. As little wonder that among the most effectual methods of making the occasion imposing and memorable he invited you—you who are representatives of the great interests and industries and instrumentalities and activities of our country—you who typify its social, political, civil, and military power—to join with him, and to all of you he returns his thanks for the cordial manner in which you have accepted his invitation. [Great applause.] He is grateful—and he has cause to be grateful—that so many gentlemen, some of whom have come from a long distance, with no little personal inconvenience to themselves, have so kindly responded to his call. He is proud—and he has cause to be proud—that those who now sit at these tables include so many foremost men of the land—foremost in arts and arms, foremost in the pursuits that illustrate and adorn and fructify the placid days of peace, as well as the deeds that intensify and symbolize the furious hours of war. He knows—no one knows better—that such a convocation, comprising so much worth and so much distinction, is a favor seldom enjoyed and never to be forgotten, and through me, again and again and again, he offers you thanks and welcome. [Long-continued applause.]

And now, gentlemen, having said this for Mr. Childs, I am sure I speak your sentiments as well as my own when I say that we think it is good for us to be here. If Mr. Childs, as none of us doubt, is glad to meet us, we are glad of the opportunity he has given us to meet him. [Laughter and applause.] We are glad to see him eye to eye; glad to express to him, face to face, the good-will we entertain towards him, the respect in which we hold his rare faculties and qualities, the admiration we feel for that concentrated and untiring energy which has so often insured him success. [Applause.] For he has had remarkable success. Not to refer to other efforts, we know that as a book-publisher he has achieved results that few besides himself could have attained; as a newspaper publisher we have this afternoon had proof that he has achieved what none besides himself would have ventured to attempt. [Applause.] I have seen it stated in biographies of Mr. Childs that for many years his most cherished wish was to obtain possession of the PUBLIC LEDGER. It was a wish not unworthy of an honorable ambition, and he has realized it to his heart's content. The LEDGER is a Philadelphia institution. Its commencement marked an epoch in our local history; in its progress it has been identified with all our local movements. At the outset it was a startling novelty; now it is a recognized necessity. How well I remember when the first number that was issued made its appearance. Though diminutive in size, it was, as this fac-simile shows, a creditable journal from the beginning, alike in its mechanical execution and its literary contents. And well it might be. Its publishers were three printers unusually skilled in all that belonged to their calling; its editor was a scholar of wide culture, a keen and bright observer, and a writer of uncommon fluency and force. Until Mr. Childs became its purchaser, two of its original proprietors continued to be its owners; until the death of its original editor, he continued to contribute to its columns. This permanence was and is characteristic of the LEDGER. The men who devised it, like the man who now conducts it, were wise and farsighted, and they laid its foundations on an enduring basis. [Applause.] They intended it should last, and not allowing any temporary inducements to swerve them from their purpose, they persevered until it was accomplished. And it is a striking example of what patient application intelligently directed can do, that an apparently hopeless undertaking, begun with limited means, under serious disadvantages, has, within the memory of many who hear me, largely enriched its projectors, and that the little obscure office in the old Arcade has been replaced by the palatial establishment—so vast in its design, so substantial in its structure, so ornate in its embellishments, and so perfect in its appointments—we have so recently visited and examined. For this last we are indebted to the munificence of Mr. Childs [applause], and while we of Philadelphia are under especial obligations for the beautiful edifice thus added to our city, his brethren of the press everywhere owe him gratitude and praise for the costly monument he has reared to the dignity, importance, and value of our profession. [Long-continued applause.]

An analysis of the life of a newspaper like the LEDGER, viewed in relation to the facts of its birth, the conditions of its growth, the forces which have controlled it, the power it has acquired, the influence it has exerted, and its general reaction on the community from which it derives its support, would be an interesting and instructive study. But such an analysis cannot now be entered on—at least not by me; for having discharged my vicarious functions, my business is to bring forward others, and not any longer to remain in the foreground myself. [Cries of "go on."] And just here I confess my difficulty occurs. With so many eminent persons around me, I scarcely know how or where to choose. But as I must begin somewhere, and as this is, in a large measure, a gathering of journalists, met to celebrate a triumph of journalism, I believe I cannot do better than ask my venerable friend, Mr. Chandler, who so long and so ably upheld the fame of our craft, and who is the oldest member of the editorial fraternity now present—perhaps now living—to favor us with whatever he may deem best adapted to the occasion. [Applause.]

To this end, gentlemen, with the expression of an earnest hope that the closing years of his well-spent life may be as smooth and happy as his earlier and later manhood was active and useful, I propose

"The health of JOSEPH R. CHANDLER."

REMARKS OF THE HON. JOSEPH R. CHANDLER, LL.D.

Mr. CHANDLER, who was most cordially greeted, said:—

Dr. Young, in talking of himself, as a good many old people are apt to do, without speaking as well as he did, said, "I've been so long remembered, I'm forgot." It becomes me rather to say, I have been so long forgotten that this new recollection of me seems startling. Indeed, I have been for these last few years so dead to society, so buried in private pursuits, that I had become quite a Sadducee in regard to my own resurrection to any public intercourse; and if I did not feel that I have a sort of personal interest in all that concerns the public press, and at least a traditionary claim to your recollection, I should be amazed at being summoned to this gathering, especially as I find myself among so many young "Pharaohs that know not Joseph." [Applause.]

Deficient as must be my remarks in aught that can amuse or instruct the assembly, I shall task its patience less if, of the few moments which I am to use, I give a portion to the expression of my profound gratitude for the kind manner in which you, my old friend and successor in business, have been pleased to refer to me and my labors; and while I felicitate you and your friends upon your success and triumphs in all that you undertake, I congratulate myself on the enjoyment of their kind esteem and on your good opinion, so flatteringly and so beautifully expressed. [Applause.]

But I am called up as one of the past—one of the rusty links that connect the old with the new; to speak of bygone times, and especially of the connection of this day's proceedings with the elder press of our city. Pardon me, or rather applaud me, if I only gossip a little, and leave speech-making in better hands.

When I commenced connection with the newspapers nearly fifty years ago, the simple hand-press, that gave two hundred and fifty impressions an hour, sufficed for all demands upon the office; but an increase of general interest and of business rendered necessary some additional means, and one new press after another was invented and used, till finally—and I suppose it is finally—came the "Hoe Press" to take its place in a newspaper office—nay, to take the place of all others, and do with a single machine, in an hour, as much as a brigade of the others could accomplish in a day.

Every pursuit in life, while, if lawful and generous, it creates agreeable association among its members, begets also a little jealousy, emulation, and rivalry; and no man in any calling ever saw a rival come into the field of his labors without an interested inquiry as to the effect which the new-comer is to have upon his share of the harvest. Business men of the same pursuits unite, indeed, with much harmony in defending and protecting the limits of their trade, but the union is only against others out of the trade. Within the circle each individual of the confraternity is watching for his own interests, and jealous of the encroachment of each brother of the same craft.

Before the LEDGER appeared there was a calm in the newspaper world that seemed to denote some coming agitation. Up to that time I had seen nothing that excited anxiety in me relative to my own interests. I could at least keep pace with others, and saw my subscription list slowly but steadily improving. But when the LEDGER sprung into existence, there was in its management and in its general appearance an earnestness that seldom fails of success, when backed by perseverance; and other schemes of a similar kind, in this city, seemed to feel and confess and submit to the supremacy of the undertaking of Mr. Swain and his associates. I felt a little anxiety, I confess, because I saw what the "Sun" was doing in New York for itself, and, always distrustful of myself, I was solicitous about the influence of this new-comer upon the "United States Gazette." Like others, I could philosophize upon the advantages of rivalry and competition. But how was this competition to affect me?

I had many friends ready and willing to aid me in their way; but there was only one business man in this city to whom I mentioned my solicitude. I asked him what he thought the effect of the LEDGER's success would be upon the large papers—of course I meant the "United States Gazette." That friend was Henry C. Carey, a man whose clear head and business habits made his opinions eminently valuable, while his warm heart would not allow him to withhold advice when he believed it would do good. "The prosperity of the LEDGER," said Mr. Carey, "and I consider that prosperity certain—the prosperity of the LEDGER will, as I think, restrain for a time your advancement. It will not draw away your subscribers, but for a time it will interfere with additions to the list. But the result will be, and that before long, that the LEDGER will educate a class of readers that now seldom see a daily paper, and they will become your subscribers."

My own experience showed the justness of Mr. Carey's opinions, and it is probable that the large papers of the city, all that succeeded, owed much of their prosperity to the influence of the LEDGER, assisted by their own enterprise and talents. For they have succeeded—succeeded beyond all that preceded them—and will, I hope and believe, continue to succeed. [Applause.]

"But," it will be asked, "is the LEDGER still only the pedagogus that brings readers to the other papers, or has it been content merely to direct the abcedarians of the lowest form?"

The LEDGER has done the work which Mr. Carey mentioned. Under its old and able management it scattered knowledge, and created an appetite for newspaper reading—an appetite which was gratified by a larger press. But in doing that it disclosed abilities for a higher office, and among the earliest results of the new reform the first great work of Mr. Childs was to take advantage of the general character which the LEDGER had obtained as a teacher, so that now, not only does it conduct the scholar to the academy, but Mr. Childs has improved and elevated his establishment into the dignity of a university. Therein he shows his mastership. [Applause.] It was much to discover the vast capabilities of the LEDGER as it was a few years ago. It was more to give those capabilities their highest direction, and secure to the public and to the proprietor, objectively and subjectively, their incalculable advantages. It was much in Mr. Swain to detect the exact wants of the people, and so to supply that deficiency as to make himself and the establishment a necessity to the community. It is more in Mr. Childs to seize upon the great work of his predecessor, and to make it respond to the new wants of the people, and to gratify an elevated taste by the very means by which that taste had been cultivated. [Continued applause.]

In noticing the contents of the first number of the PUBLIC LEDGER, a copy of which is now before us, the date seems to have escaped remark. It was issued on a Friday. Think of that. I do not allow myself to be superstitious about days and seasons, but there are many persons, and I may be of the number, who at the commencement of the LEDGER enterprise would not on a Friday have commenced a journey of any length, not even to New York, without first making their wills. Friday, sir, was, and even now is, reckoned an unlucky day. It is said, indeed, that Columbus set sail on the voyage in which he discovered America on a Friday. Well, his discovery did the world more good than it did him, and hence did not redeem Friday from its gloomy presages. But the LEDGER enterprise has improved the community, brought new honors to the press, and made opulent its proprietors. Its success has virtually added a new day to the week, and Friday will henceforth be a red-letter day in the newspaper calendar. [Applause.]

Many of us recollect when the LEDGER, in its diminutive size, was issued every morning from some obscure corner in the old Arcade, where that small beginning excited the smiles of some of the newspaper owners. Well, look at it now—not in its dimensions, but in its power to serve the public and enrich its owner. "The stone which the builders rejected has become the head of the corner." Nay, more than that—we improve on Scriptural expressions in these days—it has become the head of two corners, at least. For though the palatial structure at the corner of Sixth and Chestnut Streets is now the LEDGER Home, still there is another. You may transfer the *forms* to Sixth Street, but the spirit still lingers around Chestnut and Third. Even Mr. Childs may remove, but the old LEDGER man will be remembered for years in Third Street. There, sir, fancy will people the sidewalk with the legion of shoeless, bareheaded boys, and their echo will still rend the air with the cry of "LEDGEE," "LA-GEE," "LEGER." And though princely liberality may pour out half a million upon Sixth and Chestnut Streets, yet, for a time at least, Third Street will be the venerated Delphi of the newsboy, though the oracle be removed. [Applause.]

And to what cause or combination of causes is due all the success of the LEDGER? What has made it an institution valuable to our city with the "potentiality of wealth" to its proprietor? For this effect comes by cause. The answer is easily made. It is due in the first place to a proper estimate of public wants—to the adoption of a plan and a steady perseverance in the execution of that plan. The avowal of principles and the avoidance of party entanglements. The determination to make the paper and not its editor prominent; to have no personal obligations to repay; no private injuries to revenge through its columns. [Applause.] Boldness to argue against aristocratic claims and effete ideas, and the greater courage to breast the temporary storm of popular displeasure; to have independence enough to ask Alexander not to intercept the sunshine; and prudence enough to appeal from Philip drunk to Philip sober; liberality in views and expediencies will perfect and perpetuate what those causes have produced. [Applause.]

These made the LEDGER what it was in the hands of Swain, Abell & Simmons. These, with talents, means, and enlarged patriotism, will keep up the LEDGER to the advanced state of public opinion, and give it all the benefit of that improved general taste which it has itself wrought; while its prosperity, deserved and shared by its contemporaries, will be the occasion of unenvious felicitation in all times, as it is to-day the cause of unalloyed gratification in the most princely festivity. [Long-continued applause.]

REMARKS OF MAYOR HOFFMAN, OF NEW YORK.

At the conclusion of Mr. Chandler's remarks, Mayor McMichael said he had now a most agreeable duty to perform. Honored as the occasion was by the presence of many eminent persons from various parts of the Union, it was especially honored in the fact that the great city of New York was represented by quite a number of her most distinguished citizens—men of letters and men of action. Conspicuous among these, both in virtue of his place and his deservings, was her eloquent, wise, and upright Chief Magistrate, who had adorned the Bench over which he formerly presided by his learning and integrity, and who now, by his example and conduct, confers fresh dignity on his dignified position. He proposed the health of "HON. JOHN T. HOFFMAN, Mayor of New York."

This was received with prolonged and enthusiastic cheering, and, in response, Mr. Hoffman said:—

MR. MAYOR AND GENTLEMEN: I am exceedingly grateful for the very kind manner in which you have been pleased to greet me. Modesty compels me to declare, that I am not worthy of the good things which have been set before me, or of the pleasant words which have been spoken of me; while candor obliges me to admit, that I have enjoyed both, with a good appetite and a keen relish, even though I may not be able to digest the one or the other. [Laughter.]

I have come here to-night with entire singleness of purpose, yet in a double character—a sort of double entry for the PUBLIC LEDGER [laughter]—a kind of book-keeping which General Jackson declared he could not understand,

and which he believed was intended to defraud and deceive. [Renewed laughter.]

I come as an individual citizen, to testify my great respect and regard for our worthy host, whom I am proud to call my personal friend, and whose energy and enterprise, and intellect and integrity, have placed him in the front rank of the "men of influence" of the day. [Applause.] And I am here, as Mayor of the city of New York, to manifest the interest which our people take in everything which illustrates and tends to the development of the greatness, and welfare, and increasing prosperity of this ancient and beautiful city of Philadelphia. [Great applause.]

I am here also with a secret purpose, which I reveal to you in the strictest confidence, and which the reporters will please not to note. I am here by the way of better qualifying myself for an important part of my official duties at home—to take a lesson in the art of after-dinner speaking from your distinguished and worthy Mayor McMichael [great laughter], who, in that department, as in all others, the universal testimony of the country declares is, like Captain Cuttle's watch, "equalled by few, and excelled by none." [Applause.] Do not imagine that I hope ever to equal him; I could only expect to do it by being, like that same old watch, "set forward a quarter in the morning, and a half in the afternoon." [Great laughter.]

I hold in my hand, Mr. Mayor, a copy of the PUBLIC LEDGER, published for the first time on Friday, March 25, 1836. The distinguished gentleman (Mr. Chandler) who has preceded me has alluded to its immense growth since its first issue. It occurs to me, as I look at it, that it has not expanded any more than the national currency has [great laughter], yet I venture a prophecy that it will not contract again with the return of specie payments [laughter]; but, under the careful guardianship of our friend

BANQUET AT THE CONTINENTAL HOTEL. 71

Childs, it will continue to expand in the future. [Applause.]

In looking over it this moment, I see under the heading of "Mayor's Office," familiar words to Mayor McMichael and myself [laughter], two notices which show that Philadelphia and her Mayor, thirty years ago, were pretty much as they are now. I will read these notices as a warning to the present company, some of whom will go home late [laughter]; they are as follows:—

1st. "Two sons of the Emerald Isle were arraigned before his Honor the Mayor, and after receiving some salutary advice were discharged from custody." A word to the wise is sufficient. [Laughter.]

2d. "Robert Hare, found drunk by a watchman between the hours of eleven and twelve. *He seemed well known to the Mayor*, who sentenced him to thirty days' hard labor," &c.

For the information of all present, and by way of caution, I beg to inform gentlemen that the present Mayor is determined to follow an example of his illustrious predecessor of 1836; and *those who are well known to him* had better be careful. [Great laughter.]

Now, my friends, before I proceed any farther, I beg to express my acknowledgments to your distinguished townsman, Mr. Chandler, for the compliment he has paid to New York—unintentionally, perhaps. Alluding to the fact that the first number of the LEDGER was published on *Friday*, he said it was a day on which he would not even be willing to go to New York, without making his will. I consider that an admission that he would be willing to go there any other day, and take the risk of dying intestate. [Great laughter.] This is, I am aware, an idea of my city different from that entertained by many who live out of it; but I beg to assure my distinguished friend that he can go there even on Friday, without making a will, provided he is not killed on a New Jersey railroad. [Renewed laughter.]

Now, my friends, you perceive I have proceeded thus far under considerable embarrassment. [Laughter.] I beg you will pardon me for my very undignified remarks. I know I am among strangers. I am not only among strangers, but I stand in the presence of distinguished men, statesmen and lawyers, who do the talking for the nation [laughter]; soldiers [turning to General Meade] who have done, and will do again its fighting [great applause]; and editors and journalists, who do, or suppose they do, the most of its thinking. [Laughter and applause.] These last are the men to wield the pen which is mightier than the sword, and sharper than the tongue; who speak to thousands every day; men of power, who give form to public opinion, and direct the course of public events. [Applause.] Among the foremost of them stands George W. Childs, the editor and proprietor of the LEDGER; the man with a warm heart and a cool head [applause]; who never makes speeches or drinks wine—happy fellow he [laughter]; who exercises influence always in the direction of public good; who commands respect because he deserves it; and who gathers around him friends from every walk in life, because his hand is always raised in the interests of humanity, and not against them. [Great applause.] As a true journalist, he appreciates and understands the difference between the liberty of the press and the license of the press. [Applause.] He deals boldly with public matters, and with public men in connection with them; but he is always careful to recollect that private character is private property, owned by that most sacred of all circles, the family circle [great applause], and that the man who needlessly assails it, is as much a criminal as if he robbed the household of its dearest treasures, or plucked from it, for his own base uses, its fairest flower. [Renewed applause.] He understands, what I wish all editors in America understood, not only the power of the press, but its proper uses, and its great mission; and by his daily conduct and life declares his opinion, that the man who owns a printing-press, and can use a pen, has no more right to indite libels, and stamp private reputation, than the owner of a uniform and a sword has to cut and kill to please his fancies, or to gratify his malice. [Renewed applause.]

I know it is no easy thing in this active, busy country of ours, where everything marches to the double-quick, and where great movements are inaugurated and discussed, and canvassed and consummated with wonderful rapidity; where the editorial pen is used with a readiness and despatch equalled only by the electric telegraph; where party passion runs high, and popular feelings and prejudices surge and roll and break as waves do on the shore of the ocean; where currents and counter-currents are incessantly setting and resetting, and changing and changing again: I know, I say, in such a country it is extremely difficult so to conduct a great daily paper as to keep it always steady in the interest of truth, firm and decided in the advocacy of the right, always within the proper limits of a well-regulated liberty, and never abandoned to an unrestrained license. Yet difficult as it is, it is possible; and to accomplish it should be the aim and ambition of every conscientious and patriotic journalist who strives for the crown which belongs to an honest man. [Great applause.] There are men who fail to do it; but I tell you, he who forgets the difference between the liberty of the press and the license of the press; who assails private character, scoffs at religion, gives currency to falsehood, panders to the worst passions of mankind, goes with the public current, whichever way it turns; encourages licentiousness, advertises all manner of evil, and circulates libels, may not have visited upon him the terrors and the penalties of the human law; but society will set its mark upon him, and even while it tolerates and takes his paper, will shun him in his daily life, and leave him to pass through the world without a friend, and into eternity without a regret. [Great applause.]

I have great respect for the Press. I acknowledge its

power and recognize its rights. I would rather it would sometimes be given up to an almost unrestrained license, than to have the first fetter ever put upon its liberty. [Applause.] It should be free even though it be sometimes criminal, but it should never be criminal because it is free. [Applause.] Its power in this country is no doubt greater than anywhere in the world. Its liberty is less restrained even by the force of public opinion, and because it is so powerful and so free, it is the more incumbent on those who regulate and control it to see that its power and its liberty are used to elevate and not to degrade, to build up and not to destroy, to purify and not to corrupt, to subdue passions and not to excite them, to vindicate truth and not to advocate error. [Applause.]

It is because I believe that these views are the views of the proprietor of the Philadelphia PUBLIC LEDGER, carried into daily practice in that great and influential paper, that I have left pressing and important duties elsewhere, to pay my feeble tribute of respect to him personally at this grand gathering of his friends. [Applause.] I congratulate him on the success which has attended him on the completion of this beautiful new building, and on his bright prospects for the future. [Applause.]

I have noticed that the architect of the LEDGER BUILDING has placed upon its top for a vane an immense pen some six feet six inches long. If it be placed there to indicate that the editorial pen of the LEDGER changes to the North, South, East, and West, with every changing current, and just as the popular breath may blow it, it is a false emblem. But if it be there to indicate that its sharp and telling point is always turned in the direction of truth and against error, it is an emblem well chosen! and if it is there with this last significance, as I believe it to be, then let it remain forever, a silent and faithful monitor to him who guards the columns of the LEDGER; giving to the people an assurance that everywhere, North, South, East, and West, he will defend the truth and maintain the right. [Applause.]

And in regard to my friend who sits near me (Mr. Childs), in closing let me say, that it is my sincerest wish that he may so live, that when the Day-Book of his life shall be closed, and its many entries shall be posted in the Great Ledger of Eternity, there may be nothing written there, by the pen of the Great Recording Angel, which he would be ashamed to have recorded, or wish to have expunged. [Long-continued cheers, during which the speaker resumed his seat.]

Three cheers were then heartily given for the Mayor of New York and the city of New York.

There were now loud and continued calls for General MEADE. In reply to these, the Chairman stated that the company had forestalled his purpose by the enthusiasm manifested in regard to General Meade. He was not surprised at this. On the contrary, it would be remarkable if, in any company of loyal American citizens where that gallant soldier happened to be, his presence were not warmly recognized. Such a recognition was alike due to the service to which he belonged, and to his own famous achievements in connection with that service. Mr. McMichael then paid a glowing tribute to the army at large, and especially to General Meade, and concluded by asking the company to join in drinking to the Army of the United States, of which Major-General Meade is one of the brightest ornaments. [Applause.]

REMARKS OF GENERAL MEADE.

MR. MAYOR AND FELLOW-CITIZENS: Notwithstanding the many occasions upon which I have been received with generous kindness by my fellow-citizens, I still feel deeply the marked manner with which you have been pleased to greet my name [applause], particularly when I see around me so many distinguished men from all parts of the country, and so numerous an assemblage of the representative men of our own good city. I trust, therefore, I shall be pardoned if, in responding to the toast you have just drank, I first return you my most sincere thanks for your kind and warm reception. [Great applause.]

Gentlemen, I am called upon to reply for the Army of the United States. To appreciate the magnitude of this duty, let me ask, What constitutes the army, and who composed the army of the Union? At the close of the great war which, under God's blessing, is now terminated [applause], the returns of the Provost Marshal General's office show that there were over a million of men under arms; and the returns of the same office show that during the progress of the war more than three millions of men were enrolled for the defence of the Union. [Applause.] When, therefore, you consider the adult population of the loyal States, and see how large a proportion were at different times in the army, you will see that in speaking for the army, I must speak for the people of the United States—for, in reality, the people were the army. [Applause.] And in this great fact we find the solution of some of those problems which have so much puzzled European nations. The rapidity with which our armies were raised and organized; the success with which they were disciplined and led to action; but, above all, the order and celerity with which these great masses laid down their arms and quietly returned to the pursuits of civil life—all these extraordinary phenomena are explained by the fact that the people constituted the army. And from this fact, also, we know that there is no danger of any Prætorian band usurping the liberties of our country, or of the army overthrowing the government; because the government of the nation is their government, created and sustained by the will of the people, and the army is the exponent of the will of the people. [Applause.] And I am proud on this occasion to say that I believe the army will in the future, as it has in the past, faithfully do its duty; and perhaps I may be permitted to refer to its present position, intrusted by the legislature of the country with the most delicate and important duty

BANQUET AT THE CONTINENTAL HOTEL. 77

ever committed to any army, and to point with pride and satisfaction to the judgment and moderation with which this duty was being discharged. [Applause.]

The fact of the intimate association of the people and the army was also illustrated by the connection of the army with the press. The mass of the soldiers, being intelligent thinkers, were great readers. When I commanded the Army of the Potomac, it was determined, to avoid the conflict among agents of different papers, and to protect the men from being imposed upon, to give to the highest bidder the privilege of selling papers at a stipulated price to the men, the agent to furnish any paper called for. So great was the sale of papers in that army alone, that the successful bidder was enabled to give a bonus of fifty dollars a day. This sum was appropriated to purchasing delicacies for the sick and wounded; but so well were these supplied by the Government, Sanitary and Christian Commissions, and other associations, that, at the close of the war, as Commanding General of the Army of the Potomac, I turned over a balance on hand of ten thousand dollars to the fund for the establishment of homes for disabled soldiers. When it is considered that this large sum was only a small part of the profits arising from the sale of papers, it will be seen how large this sale must have been, and some idea can be formed of the intelligence of the army. Indeed, the soldiers were not only great readers, but their judgment and discrimination were most admirable. Being actors, and having a personal knowledge of the events of the war, they were enabled to discriminate between those journals who gave accurate accounts, and those who, led away by the impulses of the moment, would give circulation to extravagant statements for the mere purposes of sensation. And this leads me to say that, being a constant reader of the PUBLIC LEDGER, it was extremely gratifying to me to see how faithful its war reports were, and how little that journal was carried away by the temptations of the hour. [Great applause.]

My friend, his Honor the Mayor of New York, was pleased to tell us that he appeared to-night in a dual capacity. Like him, I also desire to present myself in a double character. Having responded to the toast of the army as a Major-General, I desire, before taking my seat, to say a few words as a plain citizen of Philadelphia. And in doing so, I wish to bear my testimony to the high character of the journal in honor of whose progress we are assembled to-night. [Applause.] I think Philadelphia may well be proud of the PUBLIC LEDGER, and the manner in which it is conducted. It is truly gratifying to see how fast it is gaining in favor under the energy, enterprise, and successful management of Mr. Childs, whom I am most delighted to call a warm personal friend. [Applause.] The independent and manly tone of the LEDGER, its absence from all personality and malicious defamation, its upholding the cause of humanity and religion, and its advocacy of the interests of the masses, are facts that should commend it to every good citizen, and I trust this evening will give its honored proprietor encouragement to persevere in the good course he has hitherto so well adhered to. [General MEADE sat down amid intense applause.]

After a song, given in excellent style by HERR GRAFF, of the Mænnerchor, Mayor McMichael introduced Governor WARD, of New Jersey. In doing so, he said that New Jersey had present a delegation worthy of the State—a State of which, as well for what she had been in her past history as for what she now is, he was sure all who heard him felt proud. Her Governor, one of her United States Senators, her Secretary of State, her Attorney-General, other leading and influential citizens, and many of her ablest and most respected conductors of the press, were seated at these tables; and in behalf of Philadelphia, no less than of Mr. Childs, he gave to each and all of them, and particularly to his patriotic and honored friend, Gov. Ward, an earnest and cordial welcome.

BANQUET AT THE CONTINENTAL HOTEL.   79

REMARKS OF GEN. ROBESON, OF NEW JERSEY.

GEN. ROBESON thanked the Mayor for his kind and honorable mention of his State. Those who, by constant and familiar intercourse, are able to speak of our merits, cannot but refer to the many glorious associations that surrounded New Jersey. We are nearly yourselves. From ten thousand of our families have gone the men who have stamped the impress of their enterprise upon the great metropolis of Pennsylvania. [Applause.] While trade increases the resources of a country, the real stamina is to be found in the cultivators of the soil, and in New Jersey we claim to be an agricultural people. [Applause.] Upon this occasion I desire to enlarge upon an idea broached by the Mayor of New York; that is, that the most sacred of all circles is the family circle. I will add that it is also the most influential circle, and the journalists of the day should remember that the public press can reach the home circle everywhere, and therefore it is responsible for the education of the people. When you send your newspapers into the family circles you have reached an intelligent audience. [Applause.] Our people have been thoroughly educated during the past five years, and they can now fully appreciate and understand all the great questions which agitate the nation. The free sovereigns of a free republic are your readers. In addressing this audience, sincerity of policy is the foundation of success. [Applause.] No man can be a leader of the people unless he has a deep and abiding faith in the truth of the principles he advocates. The LEDGER has a larger circulation in New Jersey than any paper published in that State, with but one exception. The speaker closed with a glowing tribute to the city of Philadelphia and the LEDGER.

The Chairman then said that he could not doubt that the admirable and witty speech of the Mayor of New

York, to which they had all listened with so much delight, had stimulated a desire for something more from the city which produced such good things. He therefore called upon the Hon. JAMES BROOKS, who was known to the whole country by long and diligent service in the public councils, and perhaps even better known by his still longer service in connection with the public press.

REMARKS OF HON. JAMES BROOKS, OF NEW YORK.

Hon. JAMES BROOKS, Editor of the "New York Express," in reply, said:—

MR. MAYOR AND GENTLEMEN: I have come here with no little inconvenience, not only as a journalist, but as one of the oldest of the journalists of the city of New York, to bear testimony to the lively interest we all feel in the profession, and in the brilliant success of one of its members, here, in our neighboring city of Philadelphia. [Applause.] The erection of so costly an architectural structure, the inauguration of such a princely palace as that we have just been visiting, for the mere purpose of journalism, is a marked event in our era, well worthy of this commemoration. [Applause.] As travellers we go over the world to visit the Pantheon of Rome, the Parthenon of Athens, the Pyramids of the Nile, or the hundred-gated Thebes on that Nile; and though the structure for the Philadelphia LEDGER is not the Pantheon nor the Parthenon, nor those wonderful works on the Nile, yet I venture to say, if ancient Roman, or Greek, or Egyptian could now revisit the earth, and see the laborious hand-work on their papyrus or parchment, instanter, by press-work transplanted by Hoe's steam cylinder machines in the LEDGER Office twenty thousand copies per hour, they would think more of this, say more over it, as an emblem of progress, civilization, and of human intellect, than even we admiring Americans feel as we enter that Pantheon, or Parthenon, or the chambers of the Pyramids, or the hundred-gated Thebes. [Loud and prolonged applause.]

Though I have said, Mr. Mayor, I am among the oldest of the Journalists, and though I am in part a contemporary of my venerable friend near by me [Mr. Chandler], with whom I served four years in Congress (I trust not differing in patriotic sentiment now more than then), yet with that vanity which still clings to youth [a laugh], I hope I may say, not yet exhibiting the signs of age, even in this not yet long life, I have seen the art of printing make more progress than any other art of the day. I began journalism with the hand-press—no cylinder, no Napier, no Adams even, no Hoe—when the little sheet was worked off by hand, two or three, or, it may be five hundred per hour, as muscular force was applied; while now, we see the ten cylinder of Hoe, driven by steam, easily working off its twenty thousand per hour, and more, as the stereotyper may double and treble the forms. Steam in every way has been the handmaid and companion of our art. When the horseback mail was superseded by the slow wagon, when the stage-coach superseded that— (and here I may interpolate, and I think I can say, what no man living can say, viz., that I have ridden all the way by stage-coach from Portland, Me., to New Orleans, thirty days going with the mail)—after all this, when Fulton adapted steam to the river, and locomotives ran like lightning coursers along the rail, our art rapidly availed itself of them, not only to gather the news, and to hurry the revolutions of the cylinder on which revolved our types, but to distribute our printed sheets, fresh and fervid, over large extents of territories, which a horseback, or a wagon mail, or a stage-coach could not have reached till the vitality and life of that news had been extinguished by the prolixity of its travels, and all would have fallen stale upon the public eye or ear. Our Hoe machines scattered our newspaper leaves as the skies often scatter flakes of snow; and the steamboat and locomotive, as the winds scatter these flakes, spread them all over the land. [Applause.] One thing more, however, was needed for us to perfect our art, and that was the realization of the Lover's Dream—the annihilation of time and space—when our Morse, the printer, seized the lightning which Franklin, our head centre printer, had affixed to the thunderbolt, and *educated* that lightning to run on his wires, into our very editorial closets, with all the news of all the earth. [Continued and prolonged applause.] Wonderful to say, we of the "far West" now gather, and print, and publish here, in America, what is done in Cairo, or Alexandria, or in the Vatican of Rome, or the Tuileries of Paris, or St. James, London, or the Schönbrunn, Vienna, as soon as the Egyptian, or Roman, or Frenchman, or Englishman, or Austrian can know it. [Applause.] All other arts seem to have been pandering to ours—Photography, Phonography, as well as Electricity; and there is scarcely a human invention which our great art Preservative does not seize upon and profit by, as we multiply the works of human genius, and diffuse them throughout the earth. The orator's or the statesman's words fall lifeless before him, but for us; and we lift even the great preacher from his pulpit, and give him hearers to hear, far beyond his altar, his chancel, the walls of his cathedral, or church.

Thus conscious of our great mission, Mr. Mayor, I trust, as has been suggested, we journalists will try not to be forgetful of our duties and responsibilities. To whom much has been given, from him much may be expected. Till within ten or twenty years, the lawyers of our land, from the superiority of their practical training and education, framed public opinion, and led the public mind; but now no profession, save that of the clergy, exerts an influence so all-pervading and powerful as the press. The people have well rewarded our energy, our industry, and our efforts for a sounder education. We no longer struggle along in poverty, or in neglect—as, for years and years, once we did—for now here, in Philadelphia, there is more than this one Crœsus before us, while, elsewhere, as here [referring to Mayor McMichael], the people give printers some of their highest political honors. Men of so much power—with instruments of so much influence in their hands, for good, or ill—must feel not only their duties to, and their responsibilities before, their fellow-men, but know, also, that when they appear for judgment, before the great Tribunal, they will be held accountable for every talent God has given them.

But, Mr. Mayor, a dinner is not the place even to point a moral, and hence I forbear. I thought I might, as a journalist, forget for a day or two the duties I owe the State, as a member of the Constitutional Convention of New York; and I therefore left Albany to-day to bear testimony here to the great interest we New Yorkers feel in this brilliant success of Philadelphia journalism, and in the personal success of my friend Mr. Childs. [Mr. Bnooks sat down amid great applause.]

Hon. JOSEPH J. STEWART, of Baltimore, was then introduced as a resident of the city which had given Mr. Childs birth, and as an early and lifelong friend of that gentleman. The Chairman paid a suitable compliment to the energy and eloquence of Mr. Stewart, and expressed the satisfaction of the company at the presence of one so near and so dear to the host of the evening.

REMARKS OF J. J. STEWART, OF MARYLAND.

MR. CHAIRMAN: After you, sir, representing the person of our host, have, with such earnest and cordial expression, welcomed us to his presence, and then with the characteristic cleverness of a Philadelphia politician veered round and thanked him on our behalf [laughter]; after your predecessor in the "Gazette," the Nestor of the American press, has so eloquently detailed the history of the LEDGER, and the changes effected in society by the cheap newspaper; after his Honor, the Mayor of New York, has described what a newspaper ought to be, impelled thereto, no doubt, by the remembrance of the highly moral and considerate press of his own city [laughter]; after one of the Republic's bravest commanders has spoken so eloquently on behalf of the army, identifying it with the people, and has characterized with soldierly frankness the judgment and moderation with which his brethren in arms are now performing the delicate duties assigned them in the work of reconstruction [applause]; there is indeed but little left for me to say, without reiterating what has already been better said by others.

I can, however, wish, sir, that all cities had as good mayors as the city of Philadelphia [applause]; and that not only New York, but every other city in the Union, should realize in their newspapers the high moral standard set up for them by Judge Hoffman, and which he thinks the LEDGER has attained. [Applause.] I agree with him that it is desirable that the press of the country should regard private character as a sacred possession, and I would not only never have the pen wielded to destroy individual reputation, but I would go still further, and never permit it to assail the life of the nation [great applause]—that nation which surrounds the press and the people alike with power and protection, and without which none of us could enjoy our rights and privileges. [Applause.]

I come from Baltimore; and I know our peaceful city is not regarded by you heavy gentlemen of New York and Philadelphia as worthy of especial consideration. Yet I think she has a right to a voice here; for both the LEDGER itself and its present proprietor were born in Baltimore. [Applause.] The paper has helped to make Philadelphia what it is, and we sent Mr. Childs over as a specimen to teach Philadelphia what a publisher ought to be. [Laughter and applause.] I have seen the original terms of copartnership entered into by the three gentlemen who founded the LEDGER. It is a very simple document, written on half a sheet of letter paper, and was signed in an iron store on Light Street, in my city. It was a small acorn, indeed, for so large an oak.

In rambling with you, gentlemen, to-day through the NEW LEDGER BUILDING, I was forcibly reminded of the old adage that "Facts speak louder than words." In the presence or the remembrance of the facts you have just witnessed, it would perhaps best become me to keep silent; for I am sure that nothing I can say would add to the profound impression made upon you by the visit to that building. [Applause.] What did we see? A palace, charmed into life as by the lamp of Aladdin, has arisen before us. Whether regarded as to its size, the material of which it is composed, or the elegance of the structure, it may truly be called palatial. The skill of the architect has combined vastness of dimension with fidelity to detail—has harmonized the useful with the beautiful; and even the genius of Art has been invoked to add grace to that which came so perfect from the hands of the artisan. [Applause.]

This temple is devoted to the art which has been truly said to be "preservative of all arts." It was therefore a great pleasure to me to see that the sculptor had been called upon to emblematize its purposes in the form of the most illustrious of his craft. [Applause.] I remember, when, upon the banks of the distant Rhine, I beheld the monument erected to the inventor of printing, I bowed my head in profound reverence before it. I could not avoid the contrast which my mind pictured of the darkness of superstition before that event, and the brightness of knowledge since. In the press, I beheld the engine of civilization. It is the teacher of mankind, the regenerator of nations. [Applause.] To-day, upon the column at the corner of the LEDGER BUILDING, I beheld the sculptured form of Philadelphia's most illustrious son; the patriot, the statesman, the sage, the philosopher, the printer—Benjamin Franklin [great enthusiasm]—the man whose reputation was claimed by two nations, but who died as he lived, a true

American. [Applause.] The figure was intended as an ornament and an emblem. It is both; and is, moreover, highly suggestive. The kite at his feet, and the pronged rod in his hand, remind us how he drew down the lightning from heaven. When asked the use of it, he answered, "What is the use of a baby?—the child may become a man." The child has become a man, and electricity is to-day a handmaid of the press, as necessary as type or paper, a twin co-worker with the press, in the remarkable intellectual progress which characterizes our era. So this statue of Franklin, embodying both, is exceedingly well chosen to emblematize the purposes to which the building is devoted. It is, moreover, a good thing for Philadelphia to have, that her youth may look up to it, and emulate the virtues of that great man. [Applause.] The calm benignity of his face reveals the humanity of his heart; the massive brow, his rare intellectual faculties; while, over the whole figure, is spread the grand repose of a character at once sympathetic and self-reliant. Franklin attributed his success, not to his talents, or his very moderate oratorical powers, but to his well-known integrity of character. He was a true man. He endeavored to be what he seemed. "Hence it was," he says, "that I had so much weight with my fellow-citizens. I was but a bad speaker, never eloquent, subject to much hesitation in my choice of words, hardly correct in language; yet I generally carried my point." Character creates confidence in all the relations of life, and this, I know, is the main reliance of our worthy host. [Great applause.] Franklin is not more emblematic of his craft than the exemplar of his life. The code of Poor Richard is the code of Mr. Childs. Nor did Poor Richard come to this city in humbler guise than our poor Baltimore boy who is your host to-day. I have been introduced to you as the friend of his boyhood—I may add, of his early childhood. As such, it is my privilege to say to you that he has been precisely what you find him to-day. [Applause.] His heart was always larger than his means, and always will be, let the latter accumulate as they may. [Applause.] There is but one thing he always despised, and that is meanness. There is but one character he hates, and that is, a *liar*. For all other infirmities he has charity; for all differences of opinion, eccentricities, and angularities, a cosmopolitan toleration. When he left Baltimore a little boy, the affectionate regrets of all his companions followed him to Philadelphia; and the attachment they felt for him was more like romance than reality in this everyday world. We are so much in the habit of making game of all that is best and tenderest in our nature, that it is left to the dissecting knife alone to lay open the heart of man; yet who is there here that does not know how good it is to have a friend? Here is the boy who has never forgotten the friends of his childhood, and who is not forgotten by them. Here is the man whom I have heard some of the Republic's bravest, greatest, and best citizens proudly claim as a friend this night. I think I can say with truth, that George W. Childs has never lost a friend. [Great applause.]

What is the meaning of it? Is there any secret about it? I will tell you what I know. He is true; and, as you are all witnesses here, he is liberal and kind. I remember that he wrote to me years ago, when we were both boys, that he meant to prove that a man "*could be liberal and successful at the same time.*" You can say whether it is proven. [Applause.] Another thing: he treats everybody in his employment kindly and considerately, no matter what the grade of his occupation. Nothing pleased me more in the NEW LEDGER BUILDING than the accommodations prepared for every department of the labor engaged on the paper—the high ceilings, the ample room, the light and ventilation. This is real progress.

Just now we are having illustrations of individual munificence, properly eliciting the admiration of the world. Mr. Peabody is the benefactor of two nations, and the pens of England and America alike have cause to thank him.

Mr. Stewart, of New York, with—(I was about to say princely, but princes do not do such things)—with the grand munificence of a republican citizen, is about to eclipse all similar benevolences in the way of comfortably housing the poor of that city, for which all good people will bless him. Our friend here is not yet rich enough to venture upon schemes like these; but we have all seen enough to know that he is a beneficent almoner of all that comes into his hands, and I am quite sure, if he ever should become as wealthy as Peabody or Stewart, he will not die full-handed. If Philadelphians want to do good with their money, they may use him as a sieve, and, by running it through his hands, find it disbursed to the individual advantage of thousands and the general good of the community. [Applause.]

I now finish my desultory remarks with thanks to you, gentlemen, and a request that you will do honor to my toast.

Here the assembly rose, and Mr. Stewart proposed "The health of GEORGE W. CHILDS," which was drank with tremendous cheers and applause.

Three cheers were then proposed and heartily given for Mr. STEWART.

Mr. McMichael here presented M. DU CHAILLU, the African traveller, with some well-timed pleasantry about the gorillas. He also spoke of the valuable aid he had rendered to the cause of science by his patient, arduous, and intelligent explorations in fields where others had scarcely ventured.

REMARKS OF PAUL B. DU CHAILLU, the African Explorer.

GENTLEMEN: I do not know how to thank you for the very kind manner you have responded to the toast to my health proposed by the gentleman presiding over this bountiful feast and splendid banquet. I cannot express to you how extremely pleasing it is to me to be among those who have met here this evening to do honor to Mr. Childs, and to show him the high regard and great esteem we all entertain towards him. Looking around me, I see gentlemen who have rendered themselves famous in almost every profession — distinguished warriors, eminent statesmen; literature, the arts and sciences, are here represented by some of their brightest ornaments; commerce by some of its princely merchants and most honorable men. Representatives from the press, of every political opinion, have come from almost every part of the country to testify with ourselves to Mr. Childs how much we appreciate his high character, how much we admire the energy and honesty of purpose which have characterized his private life and public career. [Great applause.] I am glad, also, to see so many representatives of the press, to express to them, however humble my opinion may be, the high regard I entertain towards their distinguished body.

What should we do without the press? No great wrong can be done without the press thundering about it, no charity started without the press becoming its foremost champion. I take this opportunity, which I will never have again, to thank the press for the courtesy which they have invariably shown towards me. When reviewing my books of travels, they never have inquired what were my political opinions, in order to base their judgment; they have criticized my explorations and the opinions I have derived from them with fairness and kindness, though sometimes differing with me on some points. Without the press, my works would be unknown and my travels useless. In plain words, the press has brought them into notice. I am very happy to say that the LEDGER has always been my friend. [Applause.]

Now, Mr. Chairman, allow me to thank you for the very flattering manner you have spoken of me and of my travels. I feel that I do not deserve all you have said concerning me. I am proud to be the representative of our travellers here to-night, and I thank you all, in their name, for the honor done to us in drinking to our health.

I should do violence to my own feelings, before sitting down, if I did not thank Mr. Childs for his very kind invitation, and also to assure him that this day will always be remembered by me. [Applause.]

The Chairman next called attention to the fact that Judge KELLEY was sitting near him. This announcement was all that was needed to awaken a lively anticipation of an eloquent speech; but to take from the Judge every excuse for not replying he proposed in connection with his name three hearty cheers, which were enthusiastically given.

REMARKS OF THE HON. WM. D. KELLEY.

Judge KELLEY said:—

MR. CHAIRMAN AND GENTLEMEN: I cannot but feel grateful for this cordial reception, though I am not at liberty to accept it as an approval either of my individual action or the action of Congress. The American Press is fully and ably represented at these sumptuous tables—around them the exponents of the widest diversity and nicest shades of diverging opinion have operated harmoniously, and I cannot accept the greetings of such an audience as a hearty "well done." [Applause.]

I might have been thus deceived were I less experienced. But I know something of the winning ways by which you gentlemen of the press so often discount the "sensation" which men in high place hope to produce, by announcing their purpose a day or two in advance of its execution; and I fear that you are attempting by your cheers to seduce me into a betrayal of confidence. But I am purposed to resist your blandishments, and will bluntly disappoint all such expectations, by saying at once that I will not tell you what measures my venerated friend Mr.

Stevens proposes to bring forward at the approaching session of Congress, or what that body will do on the delicate question of confiscation, or in furtherance of the needed work of reconstruction. [Applause.]

It is thirty-one years since the first number of "our paper" appeared. It was a "wee sma'" thing, judged by the papers of to-day; but it was a grand experiment, and Messrs. Swain, Abell & Simmons deserved the large fortunes which rewarded their daring and beneficent enterprise. The fact that they saw that a new and larger class of newspaper readers might be created, proved their fitness to conduct a journal which was to be characterized by its quick discernment of the tendency of events, and its labors to guide public opinion to safe conclusions. The first number tells us that four lines of stages then sufficed to carry passengers between Philadelphia and Pittsburg, but that so rapidly was travel then growing that passengers were often required to engage seats four days in advance. What a story of national expansion does that little news item tell! How would the statistics of those four lines of stages compare with those of the Pennsylvania Central Railroad!

While listening to those who have preceded me, I have acquired a new sense of the importance of the representative position with which I am honored. Congress now legislates for a broad territory that was governed by Spain in the early days of this century. Louisiana, with the west bank of the Mississippi from the Gulf to the Lake of the Woods, was confided to our care by Bonaparte when at the zenith of his power. Spain then, and subsequently Mexico, governed the golden plains of California, and the richer mountains in which their watercourses rise. And lastly Russia, as if to open the broadest possible field for the experiment of self-government by the people and for the people, has ceded to us the North Pole, and her wide territory lying somewhat south thereof. To harmonize the interests of, and provide equal laws for an energetic people occupying so large a portion of the habitable globe, is a duty such as has never been confided to a government. He who is charged with any share of this sublime responsibility may be pardoned for rejoicing at the fact that so able and independent a Journal as the PUBLIC LEDGER has been enlarged, imbued with new life, and secured the watchful care of so intelligent, enterprising, and patriotic a gentleman as Mr. Childs. [Great applause.]

But, Mr. Chairman, our territorial expansion is equalled by the intellectual expansion of our people. The sun is our artist, the subtle power of magnetism our speedy messenger, and steam, animating the iron from our hills, relieves the millions of exhausting muscular toil, reaps our fields, forges our bars of iron and steel, drags from their native beds massive blocks of granite or marble, and carries passengers and freight with equal ease over land and sea. Wealth is thus created as if by magic, and the desires of our people are ever expanding. These thirty-one years have not brought ultimate results; they have but prophesied the future. We are but passing the portals of the wealth and grandeur of our country. Hitherto our country has been a "house divided." The people of the conflicting sections have known but little of each other, and have believed their interests to be antagonistic. As the work of reconstruction, which involves most largely the regeneration of both the land and the people of the South, goes on, they will discover that diversity of pursuits begets harmony of interests in a widespread community; and we will become homogeneous. We go forth to-day an infant giant, whose future proportions or power no man may safely prophesy. [Applause.]

The projectors of the LEDGER perceived the growing interest all classes of people were taking in the daily incidents of our own and foreign life. They sought to chronicle, interpret, and apply each new fact. They thus identified their readers with them, and fortune rewarded their labors. In our host they have found a fit successor. Mr.

Childs' life has been one of enterprise. He has ever identified himself with the giant interests of our city, State, and country. Under his influence the LEDGER has expanded in size, and still more largely in power; and our whole people rejoice in its prosperity, and that its continued success justifies Mr. Childs in dispensing hospitalities worthy the Crœsus or Mecænas of the Pennsylvania press: May the day be far distant when the LEDGER BUILDING will be pointed out as the fitting monument of the enterprising and generous George W. Childs! [Great applause.]

REMARKS OF REV. DR. HALL, OF DUBLIN, IRELAND.

After a chorus by the Mænnerchor Society, the health of Rev. Dr. HALL, of Dublin, was proposed.

Dr. HALL (since pastor of the Fifth Avenue Presbyterian Church, New York) arose amid great applause, and said:—

We used to read, sir, in our school classics, that the next best thing to the performance of great deeds, is the adequate recording of them. It is not given to every man to be a Grant, a Sherman, or a Meade [applause]; but it is something to be able to present their labors in the daylight of clear and impartial history. A daily newspaper is the history of life day by day, and it goes to form the opinions that we, and still more our children, shall form of common and current events. It is common to say that "facts are stubborn things." Sir, nothing can be more manageable and plastic. You take a fact and lay it on an editor's table, and never was dough more easily shaped in the hands of a baker, than it will commonly be. Lay the same fact on the table of an opposed editor, and it does not look the same thing; the very man who accomplished it would hardly recognize it. Sir, I am glad to be at this entertainment, because I am assured on all hands that the LEDGER has endeavored to be truthful, candid, and pure as a newspaper [applause]; and I cannot but think it a most encouraging circumstance that such a career meets with this general and influential appreciation. [Applause.] The past will, I am sure, be the guarantee and presage of a useful and distinguished future. I have had much pleasure, sir, in being here, in listening to these admirable speeches, and in witnessing your power of enjoying yourselves, of which it is easy to see my countrymen have no monopoly. Not least did I enjoy the singing of *The Star Spangled Banner.* [Great applause.] In the empire from which I come there were differences of opinion as to your great national struggle, as there will be among freemen everywhere; and as civilization extends men become candid and tolerant of differences. But it was my good fortune—there was no merit in it—to believe, all through, that though the banner might be torn, there was power enough, and there was patience enough, to repair the rent [applause]; and I hope these United States may long continue magnanimous and prosperous in peace, as they have been patient and successful in war. [Applause.]

REMARKS OF GEN. HIRAM WALBRIDGE, OF NEW YORK.

General WALBRIDGE, of New York, on being introduced, said:—

MR. CHAIRMAN AND GENTLEMEN: Incidents may be overlooked and forgotten, but epochs never. Compelled by circumstances which I could not control to decline the hearty invitation to be present, when our worthy and generous host, from amidst the grace and loveliness of this opulent city, led to the altar one of its most accomplished and beautiful daughters, I determined to come, at some personal inconvenience, to this crowning epoch in his successful and eventful life, where this brilliant assemblage, comprising so many who have rendered illustrious the military and civil history of the Republic, do testify by their presence their cordial respect and their just appreciation of the untiring energy, the stern integrity, and the unbroken persistence, with consummate ability, which has marked the career of our friend, George W. Childs, until we greet him, to-night, as the representative and proprietor of one of the foremost journals in the United States. [Great applause.]

At any period, to aid in forming the public judgment and in moulding the public sentiment of a great and free people, is a high duty, fraught with great responsibilities. But how immeasurably that responsibility is augmented, at this juncture in our national progress, when, fresh from the terrible scenes of one of the most gigantic struggles of ancient or modern times, we come to lay again the foundations of the Republic on the enduring basis of public and individual prosperity—of strict and impartial justice—with universal political equality among all classes—recognizing rights that belong to all, and ignoring privileges as belonging to none, justly appreciating to their full extent the limited powers belonging to our State Governments for the administration of local affairs, but at the same time recognizing, in its broadest extent, that still higher authority which in our political system has recently removed all distinctions of caste and color, and made homogeneous, under one great federative system, all who rally beneath the flag, and recognize the supreme authority, in the Federal Constitution, of the sovereign people who constitute the power and government of the Republic of the United States. [Applause.]

To be a sentinel at such a period, on the watch-tower of public opinion, is enough to gratify the highest human ambition; and I am sure I but express the sentiment of all present when we confidently congratulate ourselves that the eminent public journal under the control of our able friend will always be wielded on the side of justice, of morality, of law and order, and in conformity with the interests and consistent with the honor and dignity of the American people. [Great applause.]

"You may have a corrupt House of Lords and a venal House of Commons, but with a free and untrammelled press I will preserve intact the liberties of the English people," was the sublime and philosophic declaration of the accomplished orator and statesman, Richard Brinsley Sheridan.

This recognition, in the British Parliament, of the strength and power of an unbought and unmuzzled press, acquires augmented force when located among a free people, where all men stand on a common political platform, where the road of preferment is open to all, and where the highest dignities and the most exalted position may be secured by the humblest in the land. [Applause.]

One of the distinguished gentlemen [Hon. JAS. BROOKS] who have preceded me, and to whom we have listened with much pleasure and delight, has been pleased to advert to the history of the early republics before the introduction of the printing press, and also to note the extraordinary progress in science, in literature, in government, and in the arts that has attended the progress and freedom of the press, in the lifetime of a single man. Whether or not the Grecian and Roman republics contained within themselves the elements of their own dissolution, or whether they fell from their inability to resist the pressure of surrounding and barbarous States, certain it is that in the absence of an agency like the press to arouse and stimulate the common mind of the nation, for the preservation of the public liberties, these republics were gradually subverted, until they crumbled into pieces, and their prospects were forever blasted by a stern, military despotism.

The right of free discussion, of large and frequent assemblages of the people, and the ability to hold constant intercourse with all classes of the community, through the medium of the press, constitute a perpetual bulwark for our republican institutions, and while that press is outspoken and independent the public liberties are guaranteed against foreign invasion or domestic insurrection. [Applause.]

But the power of the press has recently been strengthened

by the introduction of the telegraph, and our leading journals, every morning, now furnish us with the prominent incidents that are transpiring in any quarter of the globe.

While the daily press announces to us that the kings and emperors of Europe are continually assembling in their ancient capitals to strengthen and consolidate their absolute power, and to still further crystallize their peculiar forms of government, the American press is also, every morning, advising us of the steady progress of reconstruction, now happily going on, in our recently revolted States. That that reconstruction may be such as shall, at an early day, restore their citizens to all the immunities and privileges that pertain to a full communion with the national government of the United States, is, I am confident, the earnest wish of our generous host and all who have given their presence to the festivity of this happy occasion. [Gen. Walbridge was enthusiastically applauded.]

REMARKS OF MR. GEORGE H. STUART, of Philadelphia.

MR. CHAIRMAN: The call for my name is most unexpected, and quite out of place amidst so much eloquence. I have no speech to make, but I have great pleasure in bearing my testimony to the high moral tone of the LEDGER, and its corresponding influence for good among our people. [Applause.] Mr. Childs' course, in excluding from the columns of his paper everything immoral in its nature and tendency, is fully appreciated by the friends of a high-toned secular literature, and no greater evidence of this fact could be furnished than the presence here to-night of so many distinguished men. [Applause.] For Mr. Childs personally I entertain a high regard. I have ever found him ready and anxious to give his own and the LEDGER's influence in favor of every good object. Long may the LEDGER continue under its present excellent administration to greet our citizens with its fresh and ever reliable daily news! [Great applause.]

REMARKS OF MR. WM. V. McKEAN.

The Chairman then proposed the health of Mr. WILLIAM V. McKEAN, who in his response briefly sketched his knowledge of the PUBLIC LEDGER from its beginning, paying a just tribute to the sound principles established by its founders in their management of the paper, and to their business ability. Then, referring to the progress of the country and the age in all things material to the comfort and happiness of the people, to the extension of the facilities for travel and communication, to the growth and prosperity of Philadelphia, Pennsylvania, and the United States, the advance of science and the mechanic arts, he said that all these things were mirrored in the sixty-two volumes of the PUBLIC LEDGER. They form the records of the doings of a generation, and that generation the most progressive one in the history of the most progressive people on earth.

Continuing his remarks, he said it was his grateful duty to mention a name that had hitherto remained unspoken during the festivities of the evening. It was unmentioned because the gentleman referred to had placed all his friends under strict injunction not to do so. But, notwithstanding this, it was held to be a duty not to permit the company to separate without some tribute that would show the esteem in which his character is held. He would therefore, at the special and earnest request of Mr. Childs, take the friendly liberty of disregarding the reluctance of the gentleman in question, and ask the company to join in wishing health, happiness, continued usefulness, and long life to ANTHONY J. DREXEL, the friend and associate of Mr. Childs. [At this the whole assemblage rose and greeted the sentiment with prolonged and enthusiastic applause.]

The speaker then resumed by saying that in every relation of life Mr. Drexel is a noble specimen of a man. As a business man and banker, he is gifted with the highest

ability, and that ability is guided by a large and generous
liberality, a public spirit, and a freedom from small suspicious worthy of the warmest praise. In every aspect of
the event commemorated by the proceedings of this day,
his hand, though silent and unseen, has had its noble part.
[Applause.] But, speaking under the restraint of Mr.
Drexel's reluctance to be mentioned at all, he could only
say that nowhere in Philadelphia, on this continent, or on
the face of the earth, is there any one more fully and amply
a noble-hearted man, in every sense of the term, than
Anthony J. Drexel. [Long-continued applause.]

REMARKS OF MR. GEORGE H. STUART.

MR. CHAIRMAN: Notwithstanding my knowledge that
this reference to my friend Mr. Anthony J. Drexel is contrary to his own positive wishes, yet I feel that the proceedings of this festive occasion would be incomplete
without some such identification of Mr. Drexel with our
honored host and his noble enterprise. [Applause.] I am
exceedingly gratified with the remarks that have fallen from
the lips of the gentleman who has just taken his seat, and
but for the expectation that some such reference would be
made, I think I should not have been here at this late hour.
Now that it has been made, I must be permitted to endorse
all, and more than what has been said. I have known him
long and intimately, and have had extensive business
transactions with him, and I know, Mr. Chairman, I am
but echoing the sentiments of the whole banking and
commercial interests of our city, as well as my own, when
I thus publicly testify to the business integrity, the financial ability, and the large-hearted liberality of one whom
Philadelphia is proud to recognize as one of her merchant
princes. [Great applause.] Prompt and satisfactory in all
his business intercourse, eager and willing to assist by his
means and influence in every good enterprise, and yet
withal, retiring and unobtrusive, he combines in his dispo-

sition rare and valued qualities which make Anthony J.
Drexel every inch a man—a man whom to know is to love
and admire. [Applause.] The lateness of the hour forbids
me saying all that my heart prompts me to say. It is my
earnest hope that our friend's life may be long spared, his
prosperity prolonged, and his career of usefulness length-
ened out for many a long and happy day, and that finally
he may be admitted into the rest of those who love and
serve God. [Great applause.]

The Hon. CHAS. GILPIN followed in some feeling remarks, calling attention to the absence of Mr. SWAIN, the
former owner of the LEDGER, who was detained by illness.
He proposed the health of that gentleman. It was drank
with all the honors.

The festivities were continued until near midnight, and
at the close, the company separated with an expression of
kindness and respect for the host.

Fourth of July Entertainment

TO THE

Ledger Employes.

FOURTH OF JULY ENTERTAINMENT TO THE LEDGER EMPLOYES.

Two of the notable events of the celebration of the national holiday, in Philadelphia, were the dinner given by Mr. Childs to the employes of the establishment, and the entertainment to the newsboys. For the employes the tables were spread in the spacious Press Room, and seats were provided for upwards of three hundred of them, and additional seats for about one hundred and twenty invited guests. The "Newsboys' Hall" was in the "Folders' and Carriers' Gallery," adjoining the Press Room, and a table with seats for one hundred and ten of these active and enterprising young paper merchants was established there.

The Press Room, which for the day was the banqueting hall, was profusely and handsomely decorated with the national colors festooned from column to column, and tastefully gathered into clustering folds everywhere along the cornice and walls. There were five long tables on the lower floor and one in the gallery. These were spread with great taste and abundance. The following is the bill of fare, a copy of which, printed in crimson and gold, was laid upon the plate of each guest:—

BANQUET.

In commemoration of the opening of the NEW LEDGER BUILDING, southwest corner of Sixth and Chestnut Streets, Philadelphia, given by Mr. GEORGE W. CHILDS to his friends and employes, on Thursday, July 4, 1867.

SOUP.—Green Turtle.
FISH.—Kennebec Salmon.
Roman Punch.
ROASTS, &c.—Spring Chickens, Beef à la mode, Roast Lamb, Roast Beef, Cold Ham, Tongue.
VEGETABLES.—Peas, Beets, String Beans, Salad, Potatoes, Pickles.
DESSERT.—Ice-Cream in moulds, Raspberries, Soft-shelled Almonds, Grenoble Walnuts, Oranges, Candies, Pies, Pecan Nuts, Cakes, Filberts, Raisins.
Claret Punch, Beer, Lemonade, Cigars.
MUSIC.—By Hassler's Military Band.

The hour fixed for the dinner was half-past one, and the signal for proceeding to the dining-room was the playing of a grand march by Hassler's Band. As the signal was given, the long lines of the employes and their guests commenced filing along the pavements of Sixth Street and Chestnut Street, and down the stairways into the dining-room. There were one hundred and thirty-five carriers and assistants; sixty compositors and "subs," with their foremen, proof-readers, and copy-holders; twenty pressmen and feeders, with their superintendent of machinery; twenty-two folders and counters, with the night clerk; ten office clerks, with the cashier; sixteen general employes, including engineers, machinist, carpenter, watchmen, paper-wetters and turners, office boys, &c.; four stereotypers; thirty job office hands, with their superintendent and foreman; and twelve editors and reporters. These number three hundred and nine who were present, and with about one hundred and twenty invited guests, including Hassler's Band and the Athletic, Jr., Glee Club, make four hundred and twenty-nine who participated in the dinner and cele-

FOURTH OF JULY ENTERTAINMENT.

bration in the press-room. This is independent of the newsboys, who filed down the southern stairway into the gallery set apart for them, two and two, marshalled by Duffy and Hanly, two veterans, nearly sixteen years old, one of whom led by the hand young "Patsey Courtney," who seems to be the pet of all the tribe. Then came the dinner, with fountains of cool and refreshing, but not intoxicating, drinks, and instrumental and vocal music, and speech-making, and jovial conversation, and general hilarity. When the tables were cleared, the company was called to order by Mr. WM. V. McKEAN, who presided in the unavoidable absence of Mr. Childs, and addressed them in substance as follows:—

ADDRESS OF MR. McKEAN.

GENTLEMEN OF THE LEDGER ESTABLISHMENT AND INVITED GUESTS: Mr. Childs promised himself the pleasure of dining with you all to-day, but, as it sometimes will happen with all men, he has been doomed to disappointment, and I am requested to express to you his deep regret that it has so happened. It would have been one of his highest pleasures to be here to-day, and to see you all enjoying yourselves to your hearts' content. It is a part of his nature to delight in making people comfortable and happy—a great merit in any man, but with him this feeling seems to well out spontaneously, and I don't believe he could help it if he wanted to. [Applause.] This is our first Fourth of July in the new building, and you will understand by what you see before you that on this occasion he has not forgotten the workers. As the acting head of the establishment, I am commissioned by him to express his great satisfaction with the manner in which the more than three hundred employes of the LEDGER co-operate with him, and with all connected with the direction of the establishment in furthering the great objects of the LEDGER. [Loud applause.] I say this to the compositors and pressmen, editors, clerks, and proof-readers — carriers, stereotypers, carpenters, machinists, feeders, folders, engineers, watchmen, janitors, office boys, and all. To all I am commissioned to express his thanks and satisfaction. Now, let me say a word or two for those who are here and not directly connected with the establishment, as well as those who are, that it is a further source of satisfaction that this assemblage of workingmen represents a large amount of individual capital—certainly not less than half a million; that a very large number of the LEDGER employes are not only industrious, but thrifty men, who look to their own welfare, and the future welfare of their families, by husbanding their means. It is to promote this feeling among them, to encourage it in every possible way, that a great deal of the cost appertaining to this building has been expended. It is an object auxiliary to all the other objects that those connected with the LEDGER establishment shall have reason to take *pride* in it [applause]; and the best way in which they can exhibit that pride, and manifest their appreciation, is to continue their excellent deportment and conduct as citizens, heads of families, and members of the printing craft, and by taking care that what has been done here for their comfort and health, and for the sake of themselves and their families, shall not have been vainly expended upon unthrifty men. Printers are among the best paid of mechanics, and from the large annual amounts paid to them and the other employes of the establishment, there can be no reason why the private capital of the men here to-day—and which, from knowledge, I estimate at half a million—should not be, upon July 4, 1868, if we shall be spared to meet again upon that day, nearly six hundred thousand dollars. The carriers, although they do not make the highest wages, have been among the thriftiest of the employes, and the aggregate value of their LEDGER routes would sell at the Merchants' Exchange, as readily as Government securities, for a sum not less than two hundred and fifty thousand dollars, and probably three hundred thousand dollars. This shows what industrious and thrifty men can do out of even moderate wages; and it would be a high gratification to Mr. Childs, and you know it would be to me, if he could see you all following this laudable example. [Applause.]

Now, gentlemen, that is the end of a sermon that I have long wished to preach to you, but perhaps I ought to apologize to you for preaching it upon a festive occasion. You know how I have tried to impress it upon you individually, because, having been one of you, I naturally hold your interests close to my heart. On the day of the formal opening of this building, it fell to my lot to explain some of the principal objects that were kept in view in the erection of this building. It was to be as convenient a printing house as could be constructed. It was to be a wholesome place for you to work in. Then it was to be an ornament to Philadelphia. The first two of these objects were for you exclusively. You see that you have spacious, airy, lofty-ceiled, and well-ventilated rooms. This is to preserve your health, and to enable you to continue your usefulness to your families, to be effective supports to them, and to be thriving members of society.

These objects I know you will appreciate, and when the new machinery shall be erected in the room in which we are now enjoying ourselves, that will increase the present large printing capacity of the LEDGER more than *fifty* per cent. beyond what it now is, so as to get the LEDGER into the hands of the workingmen, mechanics, business men, and others, who have to leave their homes before seven o'clock in the morning. I hope you will actively, heartily, and cheerfully co-operate to that end. It will be a great point to achieve this more fully than it has ever yet been done. It should be the desire of every one connected with the establishment that the People's Newspaper, containing a condensation of the intelligence and the thought of the world, shall be in the hands of the masses of the people betimes in the morning. When we shall have done this within the next few months, we shall have accomplished a task worthy of us all, but which will be a work well befitting the inauguration of this building as the "Palace of the People's Newspaper." [Applause.]

And now, gentlemen, I have done, and will introduce to you, as one worthy of speaking for the masses—a man widely known as an esteemed mechanic—a man eminent in one of the noblest of our benevolent organizations, and whose hand is in almost every good work for his fellowmen, Mr. JAMES B. NICHOLSON. He will speak for that great outside public who have so much to do with the prosperity of the LEDGER, and whom we place first on this occasion, although it is specially the festival of the employes of the establishment. [Loud and continued applause and cheers as the speaker concluded.]

REMARKS OF MR. NICHOLSON.

Mr. NICHOLSON came forward, and, taking the stand, spoke as follows:—

This is a peculiar and proud moment for all who have felt an interest in the prosperity of the PUBLIC LEDGER; and who is there in this city that has not? The career of the PUBLIC LEDGER is more or less intimately connected with the interests of Philadelphia, and especially with the welfare of the workingmen. If we speak of the workingman in the narrow, lower sense which popular definition assigns in that sphere, we find that the LEDGER has been an instrument of good in the community. I remember well when the LEDGER's career commenced, and the suspicion with which at that time it was regarded. Its low price and easy modes of payment and its ostensible objects led many to fear that it would be instrumental of evil in catering to the passions and playing upon the prejudices of the least educated portion of the people. Nobly, right nobly have those fears been dispelled; the LEDGER in its instincts has been true to a higher, nobler humanity, and proved itself to be the true friend of the workingman. When large bodies of the people were swayed by passion, and "mob-law" was scattering destruction and death throughout the city, when good men were appalled, and brave men grew timid, the LEDGER faltered not in its fealty to the majesty of the people, but it daily asserted the supremacy of the law. Its appeals have ever been to reason, in antagonism to the passions of a mob, regardless of the pretence or the purpose under which the leaders of lawless faction arrayed their ignorant and misguided followers. The LEDGER has in this respect alone won, and it now commands, the respect of the citizens of Philadelphia.

Passing from the lower to the higher, truer idea of a workingman—that all are workers who toil either with the brain or with the hand—those who build cities and establish nations, the LEDGER has in that aspect still higher claims to public regard and consideration. Its columns have displayed from time to time the topmost thoughts of the age. Its leading articles, ridiculed as they were at first, may be referred to as brief, but comprehensive essays upon philosophical, moral, literary, or other beneficial subjects, and they have been characterized by a liberal, elevating, and ennobling spirit: they breathe the breath of a common, world-wide humanity. The LEDGER has won the love of the hopeful, aspiring sons of toil, and the indications now are, that the future will add to its claims to admiration and respect. [Great applause.]

The press, the mightiest power of modern times, is a fitting emblem of the worker. Through all its details and ramifications, from the throbbing brain of the editor to the daily rounds of the carrier, it gives evidence of unceasing, persistent, well-directed labor. In the PUBLIC LEDGER we behold an illustration of capital and labor going hand in hand and working beneficently together. Surely, then, the workers in this our work-day world have reason to congratulate themselves when journals like the LEDGER take another forward step. [Applause.]

This magnificent temple, dedicated to the good of the people and their advancement, has been justly spoken of; the provisions which have been made for the comfort and health of all connected with the establishment have been properly adverted to, and should receive fitting acknowledgment from the workingmen of Philadelphia. [Applause.] And while I, for my part, would echo and re-echo every word of praise that has been uttered or that may be uttered in relation to the projector of this building, I feel that he is worthy of higher eulogy than even that. I have watched the career of the LEDGER from its commencement; I have particularly noted its management since the proprietorship was assumed by my friend George W. Childs [long-continued cheering], and as a citizen of Philadelphia, as a workingman, as a believer in the perpetuity of American institutions, I find in the conduct of the journal itself, in the columns of the LEDGER, something that impels me to speak more highly of George W. Childs and those associated with him than I could do solely on account of this magnificent edifice which has been added to the ornaments of Philadelphia. [Applause.] That something I find in the purity of the editorials of that journal; I find it in the total exclusion of all advertisements of an immoral character from the columns of the PUBLIC LEDGER. [Applause and cheers.] For this, if for nothing else, as one of the people, I give to the PUBLIC LEDGER my unfeigned admiration and respect; because public welfare, individual happiness, and the perpetuation of American institutions depend upon public intelligence and private virtue. [Applause.]

Without further occupying your time, gentlemen, allow me, as one called upon, and permitted to speak for the *people* of Philadelphia, to say in their behalf—in behalf of humanity, in behalf of the citizens of our glorious republic, as I point to Mr. George W. Childs and his associates— behold, the men whom we delight to honor. [Enthusiastic applause.]

The Chairman then said: I deem it a duty, as well as a pleasure, at this time, to propose the good health, long life, and continued usefulness of a gentleman very dear and very valuable to every one of you. He is a gentleman that you all think of at least once a week; he is a gentleman who thinks of you to great purpose at least once a week—this is the "Cashier of the LEDGER" [cheers and laughter]—Col. M. RICHARDS MUCKLE.

MR. MUCKLE, FOR THE CASH OFFICE.

Col. MUCKLE, in response, said:—

GENTLEMEN: My heart beats within me like a sledgehammer driven by a forty-horse power engine. [Laughter.] I want you to understand, in the compliment just proposed, that you see before you what may be termed one of the "old fixtures" of the PUBLIC LEDGER, and you will therefore observe that in occupying the new building at least some of the fixtures of the old were taken along. [Laughter.] I regret my inability to fill with my voice this immense apartment, but I would be derelict to my duty if I did not respond in some manner to the compliment of Mr. McKean, who stands here to-day as the representative of George W. Childs, Esq.

For myself, I can truly say I stand here to-day a happy man. [Applause.] Not only age, but associations have made me so. When, as a boy of fifteen years of age, I made my first appearance in the LEDGER establishment, we had a little cubby-hole of about twelve by fifteen feet; and we thought it a monster concern, and so it was when we looked at the still smaller place in the Arcade. We made a move to Second and Dock Streets, and in 1840 came to Third and Chestnut, to a building that was considered a palace in those days. Even at the building at Third and Chestnut Streets, we found the necessity for more room. At first we had for the front office a room of about twelve by seventeen feet, and thought it ample. So it was for some time.

The twenty-five years I have been in the "front office" have been the happiest of my life, and I have never had occasion to regret the day I went there. And I can state that I owe it all to a good German mother. (Colonel Muckle then gave a sketch of his career as a boy in New York in search of employment, and his recall by his mother, and then his subsequent visit to the LEDGER establishment for employment.) On Saturday morning I went to the office, and presented myself to that good fellow, Mr. SIMMONS. He took me by the hand and called me his boy; and he continued to call me his boy until he vanished from this earth to occupy a place in the temple above. I have continued in the office ever since, and, as its cashier, I believe I may truly call myself the workingman's friend. [Laughter and applause.] I have never been absent more than ten days at a time, for my duties required me to put back in haste, in order, like a good general, to bring up the stragglers from the rear—(allusion to back work.) In regard to Mr. Childs—that noble man, that prince among princes—who has been proprietor of this paper a little more than two years, I wish to say a few words. My acquaintance with him dates twenty years back. I knew him in the book trade. For some time he occupied as his place of business the very spot I afterwards used as my office. I loved him from the first, and so much so that my eldest born is named "Childs." [Applause.]

Mr. Muckle referred to what he considered the great feature of the day—the assemblage of one hundred and ten newsboys, where all was joy and happiness. Here again was another evidence of Mr. Childs' kindness; and as another striking proof of his kind disposition, he would state that during the two years of the present proprietorship he had dispensed for him more money in charity than was given during all his twenty-three years' connection with the establishment. [Applause.]

The Chairman then asked the company to join in a sentiment to a man whose connection with the LEDGER was even older than the LEDGER itself, for he was the owner of the "Daily Transcript," the name of which is found still living in the sub-head to the second page of the LEDGER— a man whom he could endorse as the best mechanic, the clearest thinker, the best adviser in all matters of machinery he had the good fortune to know, WM. L. DRANE, the superintendent of the LEDGER press room. [Enthusiastic cheering and applause.]

MR. DRANE, FOR THE PRESS ROOM.

Mr. DRANE, in response to repeated calls, said that he did not anticipate being called upon for a speech, but some of the old newspaper people having learned that he was one of the oldest newspaper publishers in the city, appeared determined to bring him out. More than thirty years ago he conceived the idea of publishing a paper in this city which would give the local and current news of the day for one cent. He did not mention dates, because he was a bachelor. [Laughter.]

He had conceived the idea of publishing a penny paper from reading the glowing accounts of the success of the "Penny Magazine," and, in September, 1835, some months before the publication of the LEDGER, he published several numbers of the "Daily Transcript," for the purpose of feeling the pulse of the public on the subject of a daily penny paper. After that date the "Daily Times" was published for one cent a copy, but failed. Several numbers of the "Transcript" appeared just before the October election of 1835; but the failure of the "Times" did not deter Mr. Drane, for, in February, 1836, he commenced, and afterwards published regularly, the "Daily Transcript," until September, 1836, when he gave Swain, Abell & Simmons, of the LEDGER, his good-will and that of the "Transcript." [Applause.] The LEDGER was commenced on the 25th of March, 1836. Mr. Drane said that newspaper publishers at that time performed the largest amount of labor, as local reporter, news editor, proof-reader, and sometimes clerk.

He could narrate many events connected with the introduction of penny papers in Philadelphia, but time did not permit. The speaker became connected with the LEDGER in May, 1837, when Mr. Abell and Mr. Simmons went to Baltimore to start the "Sun," while Mr. Swain remained in Philadelphia. He closed with the sentiment: "The PUBLIC LEDGER—may its future career be as useful and instructive as its past!" The toast was drank amid great applause.

At this point the Chairman proposed "Prosperity to the Compositors, to their veteran and respected foreman, GEORGE BAITZEL, and his worthy assistant, WILLIAM SHIELDS."

Mr. BAITZEL was brought forward, and received with cheers. In response, he stated that he had been indisposed for several years and unable to attend to his duties, and on this occasion he did not feel able to make a speech.

The Chairman then asked leave to introduce a sentiment in honor of one of the most estimable classes of the LEDGER employes—the Carriers, who are a highly prosperous body of men, because of their thrifty habits, and the aggregate value of whose routes is worth nearly, or quite three hundred thousand dollars.

This was responded to by Dr. BODINE, the oldest carrier, who referred to the fact that he had been connected with the LEDGER from the time it was located at Second and Dock down to the present time. He paid a tribute to the worth of Mr. Swain, the proprietor with whom he was most frequently brought into contact. The speaker narrated incidents of Mr. Swain's enterprise in securing news before the use of the telegraph. In the transfer to the new proprietor no greater compliment could have been paid to the LEDGER itself than in the selection of Mr. Childs as the successor of those who started the paper. The speaker thought Mr. McKean had underrated the value of the carriers' routes, as they were worth at least one-third more, and were certainly largely increased in value since Mr. Childs became proprietor.

Mr. HOOVER, another carrier, being called upon by his fellow-carriers, referred to the hardships incident to the business of serving the LEDGER. In all weather, summer and winter, the paper must be delivered. Every carrier will understand the difficulty of wading through the snows of the winter before the shovels have been at work, and when it is of more importance to preserve the *paper* than the skin of the carrier. In this connection, he wished that all persons who subscribed to the LEDGER would provide a box in which the paper could be deposited, instead of being slipped under the doorway. [Applause.] The speaker also referred to the fact that the carrier is also a watchman or guardian of the people's property, for frequently in his morning journey he finds his subscribers' doors open, inviting the visit of robbers. To give the alarm is his first thought, and thus he preserves the property of the citizen. [Applause.] The speaker closed with a eulogy on the press, and a toast so highly eulogistic of Mr. Childs, that the reporter feels sure that if he were present in the city he would scarcely consent to its publication, and it is therefore reluctantly omitted by the reporter.

Speeches were also made by JOEL COOK, JR.; JOHN L. HENDERSON; R. C. SMITH, Editor of the "Sunday Times;"

Col. Fitzgerald, Editor of the "City Item;" John D. Watson, Editor of the "North American, and United States Gazette;" J. E. Jackson, and others.

The company separated shortly after seven o'clock, after a season of six hours of uninterrupted enjoyment.

THE NEWSBOYS' BANQUET.

This was the jolliest set of juveniles assembled on the Fourth. There were a hundred and ten of them of all ages, from seven to sixteen, and in all styles of costume from the neat and clean to that which was more picturesque than either; and they were of all descriptions of physical condition, from the lank and lean to the well rounded plumpness of the sturdy little chap with auburn hair and face all covered with freckles, known as "Roast-beef." They had set out to have a jolly day over the Ledger festival, and they had it. They ate and were merry, and had uproarious fun. They went through their bill of fare from turtle soup and salmon to the last items of sponge-cake and ice-cream, and had adjourned before half the grown up folks in the press room had got through with their soup. It was a part of the programme for these youngsters that an effort should be made to amuse them, and also to "talk to them like a father," but they were far too busy for that. When the manager of the establishment went into their gallery to open up this part of the ceremony, and thought the best beginning would be to assure them that they need not eat so fast, for Mr. Childs had provided plenty, not only to eat there, but enough cakes and confectionery also for them to take home to their brothers and sisters, they cut in, before he got through his first sentence, with "three cheers" for him and "three more" for Mr. Childs, and kept on cheering until he had to beat a retreat, and postpone to a more favorable time both the amusement kindly offered by Signor Blitz and his own design to persuade them to be more careful with their earnings.

EMPLOYER AND EMPLOYED.

There is always one source of pleasure in the doing of an act intended to be a kindness to others, and to produce good results to them, and that is the satisfaction of having done a thing grateful to one's own feelings and conscience. But it sometimes happens that such an act brings with it a number of other pleasures, not the least of which is to find that what has been done is thoroughly understood and heartily appreciated by those for whose welfare it was intended. An instance of this latter kind occurred to the proprietor of the PUBLIC LEDGER. For several days after the Fourth of July the employes of the establishment were quietly and secretly engaged in getting up an expression of their feelings towards Mr. Childs for what they were pleased to call his many acts of kindness, generosity, and good-will, designed to promote their comfort, enjoyment, and welfare, and, when they had it all completed, requested him, without any intimation of what was coming, to meet them in the library of the establishment to receive it. Their spokesman then presented him with an address, most beautifully and artistically engrossed, and mounted in a rich and tasteful frame. The address was signed by eleven gentlemen, representing the eleven departments into which the three hundred employes of the establishment are divided, many of whom have been connected with the LEDGER for more than a quarter of a century, and quite a large number for periods ranging from ten to twenty years. The following is the text of this gratifying testimonial, which is published without further introduction than to say that the reception of the testimonial by Mr. Childs was a pleasure as great as it was unexpected, and one that he will always look back to with feelings of the highest satisfaction:—

To Our Honored and Esteemed Employer, George W. Childs, Esq.

Sir:—The three hundred and nine employes of the

PUBLIC LEDGER ESTABLISHMENT

Desire to convey to you some slight expression of

THEIR HEARTFELT THANKS

For your great kindness and consideration for all of them, continued without intermission since you have been

PROPRIETOR OF THE PUBLIC LEDGER;

For your innumerable acts of generosity and courtesy, of which all of them have been the frequent and gratified recipients:

For your goodness of heart, your benevolence, your enterprise, and your cardinal virtues, which not only honor you, but reflect honor upon those who labor for you:

For the uniform justice with which you have ruled the PUBLIC LEDGER OFFICE—a justice always tempered with mercy—a mercy always anxious to pardon:

And, above all, honored sir, your employes desire to thank you—

For having built a palace for them to work in, a printing-house which is unparalleled in the world, a printing-office which in all its departments is the most healthy, comfortable, and spacious on the American Continent:

For all this, and more than this, that you have done for

them, your employes desire, though it be in insufficient words, to convey to you

THEIR MOST SINCERE THANKS;

And on their behalf, we subscribe ourselves your

GRATEFUL FRIENDS AND EMPLOYES,

M. RICHARDS MUCKLÉ, on behalf of the Financial Department.
JOEL COOK, JR., on behalf of the Editorial Staff.
THOS. M. COLEMAN, on behalf of the Reportorial Staff.
WM. L. DRANE, on behalf of the Pressmen, Engineers, and Feeders.
GEORGE BAITZEL, on behalf of the Compositors of the PUBLIC LEDGER.
JOHN L. HENDERSON, on behalf of the Compositors of the Home Weekly.
FRANCIS GRAHAM, on behalf of the Employes of the Publication Department.
HENRY V. DAVIS, on behalf of the Folding Department.
H. S. HUGHES, on behalf of the Stereotyping Department.
DR. J. E. BODINE, on behalf of the Carriers and Agents.
J. E. JACKSON, on behalf of the Job Printing Department.

REMARKS OF JOSEPH SAILER, Esq.

From the "Money Market" of the PUBLIC LEDGER, Monday, July 1, 1867.

Twenty-seven years ago this day, the first "money market" appeared in the columns of the LEDGER. It was penned by the same hand that writes this paragraph, and the department from that day to this has been continuously in charge of the same person; and as an evidence of general good health and close application, it may be mentioned that no two successive numbers of the LEDGER, in the time mentioned, has been published without matter furnished to that department by him. Averaging the department at one column per day, gives three hundred and twelve columns per year, and as each of these columns of close reading is fully equal to five octavo book pages in ordinary book type, we have, as the annual product, fifteen hundred and sixty pages, and forty-two thousand one hundred and twenty pages in twenty-seven years, equal to eighty-four volumes of five hundred pages each—enough to fill a very respectable book-case. Of the quality of this matter we say nothing. Our purpose is simply to show how vast a volume of reading may be gathered together in a series of years by regular daily contributions of even so comparatively small an amount as a single column per day. And, what of the number of readers of these eighty-four volumes? The productions of the most popular author in the world have probably not been so favored in this respect as has the "money-market" of the LEDGER. When this department was commenced in the LEDGER, on the 1st of July, 1840, the edition was about fifteen thousand daily; and allowing five readers to each paper, it was from the beginning addressed to seventy-five thousand persons daily; and at that rate for the three hundred and twelve publishing days of the year, the number was increased to nearly *twenty-three and a half millions!* This was for one year, when the circulation of the paper was at the smallest. It has steadily increased from that time to the present, and by the same rule of five readers to each copy of the paper (many of the copies are read by twice that number), there is now a daily audience to the teachings of its columns of three hundred and fifty thousand persons; which number, multiplied by three hundred and twelve publishing days of the year, gives over *one hundred and nine millions* as the readers of its contents in one year. Counting the average circulation of the LEDGER for the last twenty-seven years at fifty thousand daily, with an average of five readers to the contents of each copy, and we have the immense aggregate of two thousand one hundred and six millions! These figures equal the population of the world, and nearly equal the sum of our national debt in dollars; but, unlike the volume of that debt, which is steadily rolling backward, the circulation and the readers of the contents of the LEDGER are steadily on the increase.

Correspondence.

CORRESPONDENCE.

[From the PRESIDENT OF THE UNITED STATES.]

EXECUTIVE MANSION,
WASHINGTON, D. C., June 18, 1867.

DEAR SIR: I thank you for your invitation to attend the formal opening of the NEW LEDGER BUILDING on the 20th inst., and regret that engagements, already formed, will not permit me to be present on an occasion of so much interest. I can only, therefore, tender you my congratulations upon the great success which has been achieved by your ability, energy, and integrity; and in wishing for the LEDGER continued prosperity, express the hope that in the dissemination of sound principles and useful knowledge, its influence for good may remain unabated.

I am, sir,
Very respectfully
and truly yours,
ANDREW JOHNSON.

GEORGE W. CHILDS,
Proprietor of the Public Ledger,
Philadelphia, Pa.

[From the Hon. WM. H. SEWARD, Secretary of State of the United States.]

DEPARTMENT OF STATE,
WASHINGTON, June 12, 1867.

MY DEAR MR. CHILDS: You must excuse me for reluctantly declining your polite invitation, which I should be glad to accept, simply by way of showing how highly I respect and esteem you personally, and how much I sympathize with your enlightened spirit of activity and enterprise. I am, sir, very sincerely,
Your friend and obedient servant,
WM. H. SEWARD.

[From the Hon. GIDEON WELLS, Secretary of the Navy.]

NAVY DEPARTMENT,
WASHINGTON, June 10, 1867.

DEAR SIR: I regret my inability to accept your polite invitation to be present at the opening of the NEW LEDGER BUILDING, on Thursday, the 20th inst.; but other duties detain me here.

Although unable to participate in the ceremonies of inaugurating your new building, I sincerely congratulate you on the success which the occasion indicates to yourself personally, and to the journal itself.

The course of the LEDGER, its moral and political bearing, and the ability, independence, and fairness which its columns have generally displayed, I have admired.

It is a subject of special commendation, that while the LEDGER has ably vindicated the great principles of the Constitution, maintained the integrity of the Union, and asserted the rights of the Federal Government, the rights of the States, and the rights of man, it has been exempt from that illiberal and ungenerous partisanship which so frequently disfigures our public journals.

With my best wishes for your continued success,
I am, very respectfully,
MR. GEO. W. CHILDS. GIDEON WELLES.

CORRESPONDENCE. 125

[From the Hon. E. M. STANTON, Secretary of War.]

WAR DEPARTMENT,
WASHINGTON, June 10, 1867.

MR. GEO. W. CHILDS.

DEAR SIR: The acknowledgment of your kind invitation has been delayed in the hope that I might be able to accept it; but I regret to find that I shall not be able to enjoy that pleasure. With many thanks for your attention, and good wishes for the continued prosperity of the LEDGER,

I am, yours truly,

EDWIN M. STANTON.

[From the Hon. MILLARD FILLMORE, Ex-President of the United States.]

BUFFALO, June 12, 1867.

GEO. W. CHILDS, ESQ.

DEAR SIR: I am honored by your cordial invitation to be present at the opening of the NEW LEDGER BUILDING, on the 20th of June inst., and I can assure you that it would give me great pleasure to accept it, but I regret to say that my engagements will prevent.

It is now more than nine years since I was last in Philadelphia, but report says that the building which is about to be opened, and for which Philadelphia is indebted to your enterprise and liberality, is not only an ornament to the city, architecturally, but one of the largest and most complete printing establishments that has ever been erected in this country.

Many years since, the PUBLIC LEDGER used occasionally to fall under my observation, and it seemed to me to be a remarkably well-conducted paper; and I am happy to infer that it has been profitable to its proprietor; for in this, honesty and enterprise have their reward.

I am, with great respect,
Truly yours,

MILLARD FILLMORE.

[From General Grant.]

HEADQUARTERS ARMIES OF THE UNITED STATES,
WASHINGTON, D. C., June 18, 1867.

G. W. CHILDS, Esq.

DEAR SIR: I regret that an engagement to be at Gettysburg, Pa., the very day for which I am indebted to you for a most cordial invitation to dine with you in Philadelphia, will prevent my acceptance.

With great respect,
Your obedient servant,
U. S. GRANT, General.

[From Chief-Justice Chase to Dr. Elder.]

RALEIGH, NORTH CAROLINA, June 12, 1867.

MY DEAR SIR: Some days have passed since I received your note requesting me to be present at the dinner with which our friend Mr. Childs intends to distinguish the opening of "the NEW LEDGER BUILDING."

I should be very glad to be one of his guests, and to congratulate him personally on the event he celebrates. But my duties will detain me in warmer latitudes.

His brilliant business career is marked all along by achievements impossible to any one not endowed with uncommon powers and energies. The new building will only mark the latest stage of his career. Other stages and other achievements are before him. I sincerely wish that his future may be crowned, like his past, with successes equal to his desires.

And may he long live to enjoy the present respect and good-will which his generous spirit and upright life, far more than his successes, draw to him, as the magnetic mountains draw ships—not, however, like them, to wreck.

Yours sincerely,
S. P. CHASE.

WM. ELDER, M. D.

CORRESPONDENCE. 127

[From the Hon. S. P. Chase, LL D., Chief Justice of the Supreme Court of the United States.]

WASHINGTON, June 8, 1867.

MY DEAR MR. CHILDS: My duties here will not permit me to accept your kind invitation to be present at the opening of the NEW LEDGER BUILDING; but I pray you to accept my sincere congratulations on the event. Long may you enjoy the prosperity you have so honorably won, and may it ever be identified, as heretofore, with the welfare of the great city in which you live.

If I could be with you, and were at liberty to make a speech, my theme should be: The Pen, the Telegraph, and the Press—the triple alliance that rules the world.

Yours, very truly,

S. P. CHASE.

GEO. W. CHILDS, ESQ.

[From the Hon. W. Dennison, late Postmaster-General of the United States.]

COLUMBUS, OHIO, June 21, 1867.

MY DEAR SIR: I need not assure you of my disappointment in not being of the party of your friends to inaugurate, with you, the opening of your magnificent building, yesterday afternoon, which is not more an ornament to your city than a monument of your eminent and well-deserved success in life.

Let me make to you my sincere congratulations on the completion of your building, and my warmest wishes for your future prosperity.

Accept my thanks for your kind remembrance of me, and believe me,

Truly yours,

W. DENNISON.

THE PUBLIC LEDGER BUILDING.

[From Major-General GEARY, Governor of Pennsylvania.]

STATE OF PENNSYLVANIA,
EXECUTIVE CHAMBER, HARRISBURG, PA., June 19, 1867.

GEORGE W. CHILDS, ESQ.

MY DEAR SIR: Few things would afford me more gratification than to be free to accept your flattering invitation to meet yourself and distinguished guests at the inauguration ceremonies of the NEW LEDGER BUILDING on the 20th inst. The pride and admiration that every citizen of this Commonwealth especially must entertain for an enterprise commencing in obscurity and being apparently insignificant in all its bearings, which in a few years, by prudent management, integrity in its business arrangements, persevering industry, untiring energy, devotion to the true interests of the community it proposed to serve, combined with skill, talent, genius, and all the requisites for success, could be made to assume its present magnificent proportions, would of themselves be more than sufficient to create the desire to be present on the occasion referred to, not only to take part in the interesting ceremonies, but to aid in doing honor to the gentleman who has contributed so largely to this grand result.

But, were you present in the executive chamber a few days to observe the vast amount of business requiring immediate attention, you would readily perceive how difficult it is for me to anticipate in advance a day of leisure, or fix upon a period when it would be prudent to be absent from the scene of official labor. And as it has been the invariable and inviolate rule of my life never to defer until the morrow that which should be done to-day, or to seek personal gratification at the expense of public duty, it so happens that my presence is required at Gettysburg to meet General U. S. Grant, and the representatives of the eighteen States whose loyal dead are interred in the National Cemetery at that place, at the very time it would afford me so much pleasure to mingle with your honored guests and join with them in their well-merited and hearty congratulations of the enterprising proprietor of the PUBLIC LEDGER.

Although but a boy at the time, I distinctly recollect the first issues of your paper. The obscurity from which it issued and its diminutive size gave no earnest of its present mammoth dimensions and immense public utility. But even then a careful observer could perceive that the little bantling possessed the proper spirit, and contained within itself the true elements of success. Conducted upon the most economical principles, its business managed with strict regard to honesty and justice, supplying a want that had long been felt by the masses of the community, avoiding all partisan entanglements and personal bickerings or aspersions, its news carefully selected and always reliable, its freedom from everything unchaste or unfit for the family circle, and its editorials the evident productions of a vigorous intellect and powerful pen, it soon commended itself to the general public, and gradually grew in favor, strength, and power, until it reached its present magnitude, and has become an absolute necessity.

In contemplating the unprecedented prosperity of your noble and splendid establishment, the mind is unavoidably carried back to the time of its incipiency, and to reflect upon the wonderful progress that genius, talent, and science have made in that brief period.

Excuse the length of this communication. I purposed simply to excuse my absence from your proposed festival, and to testify my approbation of your industry, skill, and zeal, as well as your princely munificence in constructing a building for your business purposes that is an ornament to the city of Philadelphia and a credit to the State, and in completing a printing establishment equalled in all its appointments, adornments, comforts, and grandeur by none other in the world.

With high respect,
Your friend and obedient servant,
JNO. W. GEARY.

[From the Hon. MARCUS L. WARD, Governor of New Jersey.]

STATE OF NEW JERSEY, EXECUTIVE DEPARTMENT,
TRENTON, June 10, 1867.

GEORGE W. CHILDS, ESQ.,
Proprietor of the Public Ledger.

DEAR SIR: It will give me great pleasure to accept your kind invitation to be present at the ceremonies attending the inauguration of your NEW LEDGER BUILDING; and I shall be especially pleased if, by my presence upon that occasion, I can testify my respect for the high character and honorable principle which have so pre-eminently marked your editorial life. To have been the proprietor and responsible editor of a paper which, like the LEDGER, has established, and for so many years sustained, a character for dignity, courtesy, and morality, and for strict adherence to the principles of truth, is an honor of which the most fortunate might be proud. The greatly increased circulation of your paper—its almost unprecedented success—is but a proof that such qualities are appreciated by the public. Your beautiful and costly building, which I have already seen in course of construction, is but the fitting result of so successful an enterprise. I doubt not that the LEDGER will continue to flourish in the future as it has in the past, and prove a great source of benefit to yourself, as well as to the public. Very truly yours,

MARCUS L. WARD.

[From Major-General SCHENCK, Member of Congress from Ohio.]

WASHINGTON, June 13, 1867.

MR. GEO. W. CHILDS.

MY DEAR SIR: I must be content with the expression of my regret, that I cannot share in a festivity which is to mark another of those magnificent and successful enterprises which illustrate the growth and prosperity of your beautiful city.

Very respectfully and truly yours,

ROBERT C. SCHENCK.

[From the Hon. Thomas Swann, Governor of Maryland.]

STATE OF MARYLAND, EXECUTIVE DEPARTMENT,
ANNAPOLIS, June 27, 1867.

My Dear Sir: I have read the account of the proceedings which took place at the opening of the NEW LEDGER BUILDING, to which you did me the honor to invite me, and cannot forego the pleasure of expressing to you my gratification at the appreciation universally expressed on that occasion of your high character as a journalist, and the well-merited success which has attended your past career. In the bitterness of feeling which has sometimes attended the progress of the press in this country and elsewhere, it is refreshing to look back upon the manly and generous spirit which has always marked your connection with it, holding out an example which cannot fail to be useful to all who are laboring in the same field.

As the Executive of the State of Maryland, I should have felt highly complimented in being present, to have participated in the cordial expressions of your distinguished friends, besides the particular gratification it would have afforded me as a personal friend in contributing my part in doing you honor as a Marylander who has elevated the dignity of his vocation by enlarged enterprise, impartial justice, and practical intelligence.

Permit me to offer you my sincere congratulations on the great success of your entertainment, and to assure you of the high regard and esteem with which I am

Yours, most truly,

THOS. SWANN.

Geo. W. Childs, Esq.

[From the Hon. Simon Cameron, U. S. Senator from Pennsylvania.]

United States Senate Chamber,
Washington, July 8, 1867.

My Dear Friend Childs: Your invitation to join in the inauguration ceremonies of the New Ledger Building reached me in the midst of active preparations for a trip to Kansas over the Union Pacific Railroad. Although I was eager and anxious to go upon this excursion half-way across the Continent, I could not suppress a feeling of keen disappointment that, in gratifying that wish, I was forced to forego the pleasure of meeting you, and joining you and your friends in the festivities which were to mark your inauguration of the magnificent Printing House of the Ledger.

My warm impulses for everything which benefits the working-man, and my pride in everything which reveals the growth and the prosperity of Pennsylvania, made me specially anxious to be present at your banquet, but, in addition to these inducements, I had the stronger one of active, practical sympathy with the object and occasion of your meeting. I have learned the trade of printer; I have labored at it for my daily bread. I have edited and owned newspapers, and I have carefully thought over the incalculable influence of the public press. I was in full sympathy with the workmen, the editors, the proprietor, and the guests, for in my life I have filled all the parts at different periods.

Our country abounds with evidences of great successes. In the department of current literature, but especially in the daily newspaper, we have seen amazing results. Men now living can trace your career by a comparison with what the best of our daily newspapers were forty years ago. In New York a wonderful development of skill and energy has been shown; but in no city of the Union has there been such a transcendent success in the newspaper world as the Philadelphia Ledger.

The success of your newspaper has something in it peculiar and interesting. It is the direct continuation of the first effort made in this or any other country to print and sell a newspaper for a penny, an amount insufficient to pay for the white paper on which it is printed. It has thus popularized the daily paper, and, more than any other engine, educated the masses in the duties of citizenship. Who can measure the effect for good which has flowed directly from this fact? Every man of sense knows that our only safety as a government consists in educating the mass of the people up to a standard of such excellence that they will not only know how to make laws, but be masters of that higher knowledge which enables them to obey the law.

Foremost, then, in this good work, I place the LEDGER, your predecessor Mr. Swain, and *you*, Mr. Childs, its present proprietor. To you belongs the honor of having done much, and the responsibility for much yet to be done. As I fully and cordially approve of your past course, so do I look hopefully to the manner in which you will fulfil the remaining duties of your high calling. And as I have been your friend heretofore, so will I continue to be your friend, your supporter, and your admirer.

Please accept my regrets that I could not meet you, and believe me, as ever,   Yours, most truly,

SIMON CAMERON.

[From General C. E. PHELPS, Member of Congress from Baltimore City.]

BALTIMORE, June 7, 1867.

GEORGE W. CHILDS.

MY DEAR SIR: It is needless for me to assure you how highly I appreciate the honor of being designated as one of your friends on an occasion so honorable to you, and so significant to your dashing enterprise and deserved success. You may certainly rely upon my presence.

Very truly yours,

CH. E. PHELPS.

[From the Hon. A. G. CATTELL, United States Senator from New Jersey.]

MERCHANTVILLE, N. J., June 13, 1867.

MY DEAR MR. CHILDS: I have the honor to acknowledge the receipt of your invitation to attend the opening ceremonies at the NEW PUBLIC LEDGER BUILDING on the 20th inst. I shall be most happy to avail myself of the opportunity to signify my high appreciation of the character of the LEDGER, and also my great personal regard for you individually.

The LEDGER, from its very commencement, has been a great power in Philadelphia, and successful beyond the most sanguine expectation of its friends. That its success will be increased, and its power augmented by the wisdom and energy of your management, I do not doubt; and I predict for you and it a career of prosperity and usefulness.

In regard to your request that I should reply to the toast in honor of New Jersey, I beg to say that, as our excellent Governor will probably be present, it would manifestly be proper that he should respond to the sentiment in honor of the State over which he so worthily presides. Yours, truly,

ALEX. G. CATTELL.

[From Hon. GEORGE S. HILLARD, LL. D., United States District Attorney for Massachusetts.]

BOSTON, June 10, 1867.

MY DEAR MR. CHILDS: Be assured that it gives me always the greatest pleasure to hear of your happiness and prosperity, which indeed are the natural result of your qualities of mind, heart, and character. I can only wish that your future may be like your past.

Yours faithfully,

G. S. HILLARD.

[From Major-General Chamberlain, Governor of Maine.]

STATE OF MAINE, EXECUTIVE DEPARTMENT,
AUGUSTA, June 12, 1867.

GEO. W. CHILDS.

MY DEAR SIR: I beg to express my grateful sense of the honor you do me by your invitation to be present on the occasion of the opening of the NEW LEDGER BUILDING, and I exceedingly regret that I cannot make such arrangement of my official duties as to allow me the great pleasure of thus renewing my association with gentlemen whom I so much honor and esteem.

Be pleased to accept the assurance of the interest I feel in every indication of your prosperity, and of the pleasure it would give me to be able to participate in the festivities of the occasion to which you have so kindly invited me.

With sincere regard,
Your friend and servant,
G. L. CHAMBERLAIN.

[From the Hon. REVERDY JOHNSON, LL. D., United States Senator from Maryland.]

BALTIMORE, June 13, 1867.

Mr. REVERDY JOHNSON much regrets that engagements beyond his control deprive him of the pleasure of Mr. Geo. W. Childs' invitation for the 20th instant. Mr. Johnson would have been much gratified in being present on an occasion so indicative of the prosperity of the LEDGER, and in uniting with the friends of the editor in testifying his admiration of the manner in which his paper has been conducted, ever abstaining from personal and reckless attacks, and always aiming to elevate the private and political character of its readers.

[From Commodore Turner, United States Navy.]

UNITED STATES NAVY YARD,
PHILADELPHIA, June 20, 1867.

MR. GEO. W. CHILDS.

MY DEAR SIR: I was particularly sorry that circumstances obliged me to leave my place at your magnificent banquet before I had an opportunity of replying to the Navy toast, as I was ready, and wanted to say something in my humble way of the close and cordial relations which bind the Navy of the United States to the press—how we have been cheered through this whole war by the generous acknowledgments of the press of the country, of our services, and especially the LEDGER. But it is now too late to make more than a brief allusion to it. When did the press ever fail to recognize, to commend, and to applaud an act of gallantry of one of our profession? When did it ever fail to receive with open arms a gallant officer returning from a field of brilliant achievements? and, on the other hand, when did it ever fail to hold up to a nation's scorn the craven dastard who shrunk from his duty in the hour of danger? I say much less here upon this subject than I should have done, if it had been my good fortune to have been able to speak for the Navy at the dinner, and pass at once to the dinner itself. I congratulate myself on having been there, for, having travelled all over the world, occasionally entertained by the first dignitaries of foreign lands—having had a very enlarged opportunity of contrasting memorable and magnificent entertainments with each other, I unhesitatingly say, that I was startled by the brilliancy, the taste, the splendor, and entire success of your *fête*, and that it far exceeded anything of the kind I ever saw or participated in; and the first thought that seized my mind was—who is the author of all this? Was it some lordly aristocrat or titled scion of an ancient house, with its revenues and retinues? Nay, it was no such thing! but a plain, modest, humble man of energy, activity, intelligence, and practicability; self-made, not yet having reached the meridian of life; who had vaulted, by his solid merit, into a commanding position of wealth, influence, and consequence, by his own exertions alone—a type of a class of men who seem, more than to any other, to belong to this country, where the mind and the energies, and the ingenuity and industry of man are given full scope to develop themselves as man will decide for himself.

I congratulate you, my dear sir, upon this great occasion, and I feel proud, as an American, of your birthright as a citizen of our great and common country, and I feel proud to be the friend of the man who has, by his own merit, advanced himself to a position which, without hereditary privileges of any sort, any man might be proud of.

I am, my dear Mr. Childs, with the best wishes for your prosperity and happiness in life,

Your friend,
T. TURNER.

[From the Hon. A. H. Rice, Member of Congress from Massachusetts and Ex-Mayor of Boston.]

Boston, June 15, 1867.

My Dear Mr. Childs: I thank you very much for honoring me with an invitation, and should need no inducements to accept it, if circumstances permitted.

You are sure of a splendid occasion, and you have my best wishes for the continuance of the extraordinary success which has hitherto rewarded your sagacity and enterprise. I am, dear sir,

Very truly yours,
ALEX. H. RICE.

[From Rear Admiral CHARLES STEWART, United States Navy.]

BORDENTOWN, N. J., July 16, 1867.

MY DEAR MR. CHILDS: Since receiving the "papers" you did me the honor to transmit me, I am filled with more regrets at my inability to have been present at the opening ceremonies, and cannot let the occasion pass without offering you my congratulations on the great success you have achieved through your enterprise and energy in establishing a building so systematic and perfectly arranged for the future issuing of the PUBLIC LEDGER.

You, my dear sir, have erected a lasting monument to your genius and generosity, and in the internal arrangements you have established an example for the benefit of all publishers to follow, in studying the comfort and convenience of the employes of their establishments.

In accomplishing your object you have contributed very largely to the embellishment of my native city, and particularly so to the great "Square" and "Hall of Independence;" but when and where, my dear sir, are we to look for a similar achievement in the improvement of the "Square" itself? This we must leave to hope and to time; but I trust the time will come when, in imitation of your good example, there will be found similar buildings on the "Square," which will constitute the "watch-towers of liberty" around that noble "Hall," from the belfry of which, on July 4th, 1776, issued the tocsin of Independence as declared by our "Revolutionary Fathers," the descendants of whom are now receiving the meed of praise from surrounding nations.

Accept the best wishes for your future success of this noble undertaking, of

Your friend,

CHS. STEWART.

CORRESPONDENCE.

[From Dr. OLIVER WENDELL HOLMES.]

BOSTON, June 10, 1867.

DEAR MR. CHILDS: Although denied the pleasure of being with you at the house-warming which threw open your noble edifice, I must be allowed the privilege of sending you my most cordial felicitations. I know something of the structure you have raised, and I look upon it not merely as a triumph of your own enterprise and talent, but as one of those historic monuments which will tell posterity to what the tide of popular intelligence had risen in our time.

This building, with all it represents, is not a mere local product, nor an index only of the taste, and culture, and liberality of the citizens of Philadelphia. No great success in this country can be purely local. There are no walls to our cities, and everything which transcends a certain measure of superiority makes itself national in so doing. Broadway and Chestnut Streets are national highways rather than common city thoroughfares. Your fellow-citizen (if such you still call him), the great General, has the freedom of all our municipalities, and is at home everywhere from the St. John's to the Rio Grande. The great LEDGER constituency, scattered all over the Union, claims a stone in your edifice for each group of its units, as fairly as each of the States which sent a block of granite or marble to help build the Barmecide monument at Washington, claims its share in that potential structure. We who drink from the fountains of Croton or Cochituate claim to be part owners and co-tenants with you who fill your cup from the chalice of the nymphs of Fairmount. Each coral insect helps to build the reef, and every one whose name is on the books of the LEDGER has a hand in raising this pile of branching and flowering stone planted in the ocean stream of life flowing through the channels of a vast city.

Some build upon sand, and some build upon rock. Your

edifice rests on solid stone, and below that upon honest gravel. But there is something deeper than either of these, which is its true foundation—a broad stratum of public intelligence, on which its corner-stone is laid, and which bears up the massive wall of the whole fabric. May it stand as long as its foundation shall endure! Health and prosperity to him who, in building up his own fortunes, has enriched and adorned his native land; and a long and happy life to the generous host, whose headquarters are henceforth in this magnificent Palace of Letters! I am, dear Mr. Childs,

Faithfully yours,
O. W. HOLMES.

[From Henry Wadsworth Longfellow, the Poet.]

Cambridge, June 6, 1867.

Mr. Geo. W. Childs.

My Dear Sir: With many thanks for this token of your regard, and best wishes for your success,

I remain, yours truly,
HENRY W. LONGFELLOW.

[From Ralph Waldo Emerson, Esq.]

Concord, June 15, 1867.

George W. Childs, Esq.

Dear Sir: It would give me great pleasure, I doubt not, to see the inauguration of the New Ledger Building on the 20th inst., and to meet you and your friends at dinner, in obedience to your invitation. But these liberties and pleasures are not for me, at this time, to be so much as hoped for. A series of engagements quite imperative hold me at home all this month and longer. Meantime, I wish all good influences and effluences to the New Ledger Building, and lasting prosperity to its enterprising and friendly proprietor. With great regard, yours,

R. W. EMERSON.

[From the Hon. George Bancroft, LL.D., the Historian.]

NEW YORK, June 15, 1867.

MY DEAR MR. CHILDS: It would give me unmingled pleasure to witness your proud enjoyment on taking possession of your new building; but my destiny leads me in another direction, and I am compelled to decline the invitation with which you have honored me.

I am ever, my dear sir,
Very truly yours,
GEO. BANCROFT.

[From FRANCIS LIEBER, LL.D., Professor in Columbia College, New York.]

NEW YORK, June 19, 1867.

MR. GEO. W. CHILDS.

DEAR SIR: Until late last evening I had hoped to be able to join you and your guests to-morrow at the opening of the NEW LEDGER BUILDING, but I am sorry to say I am now unavoidably prevented from enjoying that pleasure. The loss is mine. Do you wish me to give you a sentiment? I give in good earnest:—

Let every one who directs a journal hourly remember the power which a paper has naturally come to wield for good or evil, and opposite to the Individual—the tremendous Power of Repetition.

A sentiment ought to be of a certain brevity, else I would go on with this subject; but let me add this, that as we have Medical Ethics, and Legal and Commercial Ethics, I have long taught that we should have Literary Ethics—a very wide field—and a branch of these ought to be Newspaper Ethics. At some meeting of editors a committee ought to be appointed to report a code of Journalistic Morals.

May you enjoy yourself, and your wine be cool! Weather and Waterloo Reminiscences make it very warm.

Very truly yours,
FRANCIS LIEBER.

[From Hon. ROBERT C. WINTHROP, LL. D., of Massachusetts.]

NEW YORK, June 11, 1867.

GEO. W. CHILDS.

MY DEAR SIR: Accept my best thanks for your obliging invitation for the 20th instant. I sail for Europe to-morrow, and shall thus lose the opportunity of participating in the festivities which you propose for the opening of your New Building. But I offer you my hearty congratulations on the success of the literary enterprises in which you have engaged, and my sincere wishes for their still greater success in the future.

Believe me, dear sir, with great regard,
Your friend,
ROBERT C. WINTHROP.

[From Major-General PATTERSON.]

1300 LOCUST ST., PHILADELPHIA, June 14, 1867.

MY DEAR SIR: It is with great pleasure that I accept the invitation to be present at the formal opening of the NEW LEDGER BUILDING on the 20th instant, and to dine with you at the Continental on the same day.

The public spirit which has caused the erection of so magnificent a building is certainly a just cause of pride, not only to yourself, but to the city of Philadelphia.

The building itself is a monument to the grateful appreciation of a discerning public of the efforts of a man, in the purity of his intentions, to furnish daily information, within the reach of all, through the medium of a paper on the pages of which even the most fastidious or delicate would vainly seek for cause of reproach.

With many wishes for your success,
I remain, my dear sir,
Very respectfully and truly, your friend,
R. PATTERSON.

GEO. W. CHILDS, Esq., Philadelphia.

[From Professor JOSEPH HENRY, LL. D., Secretary of the Smithsonian Institution, Washington, D. C.]

SMITHSONIAN INSTITUTION,
WASHINGTON, June 12, 1867.

GEO. W. CHILDS, ESQ.

MY DEAR SIR: I beg to assure you that I highly appreciate your kind remembrance, and shall earnestly hope that you may long continue to enjoy the prosperity which you so richly deserve, from your talents, enterprise, industry, and integrity; and that your New Building may be renowned as a temple devoted to the advancement of our country in morality, intelligence, and refinement.

I remain, very truly,
Your friend and servant,
JOSEPH HENRY.

[From STEPHEN COLWELL, LL. D., Author of various works on Political Economy, &c.]

PHILADELPHIA, June 17, 1867.

GEO. W. CHILDS.

MY DEAR SIR: I accept with pleasure your invitation to dine with the friends of the PUBLIC LEDGER, and wish I could in some more effectual way evince my sense of the firmness, discrimination, and energy you have displayed in the management of a journal so important as yours. The LEDGER has an immense audience; it goes to the masses—the bone and sinew of society. How thankful we should be that it undergoes a supervision so faithful, so discreet and patriotic as that which you give it! The more we have to fear from the acknowledged venality of the press, the more reason for gratitude to those who, like yourself, resist practices so destructive of public virtue and social confidence. Trusting that the LEDGER may long continue to grow in usefulness and popularity,

I am, very truly, your friend,
STEPHEN COLWELL.

THE PUBLIC LEDGER BUILDING.

[From GEORGE WILLIAM CURTIS, Esq.]

ALBANY, N. Y., July 8, 1867.

MY DEAR MR. CHILDS: I was very sorry that my duties at the Constitutional Convention here prevented my accepting your kind invitation to the great newspaper jubilee. Yet I might perhaps have wisely run away to you, for it is the newspapers, rather than conventions, which make governments and constitutions. They, more than any other influence, mould public opinion, which is, in this country, and at last in all countries, really the government; and it is to them that the legislators look for the encouragement or censure of their work.

In this country we are all politicians, and the newspaper is the great political school. How gladly, therefore, should I have met so illustrious a body of teachers as that you assembled at your feast! How profound, also, is my sense of their power and responsibility! Louis Napoleon's summer guests, emperors, sultans, and kings though they are, are not truly so significant a company as yours. And as this feeling of the essential dignity and influence of the editorial profession increases, may we not hope that the sense of its responsibility will deepen? If the newspaper is the school of the people, and if upon popular education and intelligence the success and prosperity of popular government depend, there is no function in American society which requires more conscience as well as ability.

I am very sure that the speeches which celebrated the festival were not sermons like my letter. If they had been, the table would have groaned in a very different manner from that of which I read the story.

Yours, very truly,
GEORGE WILLIAM CURTIS.

[From JAMES PARTON, Esq., Author of the Lives of Franklin, Aaron Burr, Andrew Jackson, &c.]

NEW YORK, June 7, 1867.

GEO. W. CHILDS.

MY DEAR SIR: I have received your note of yesterday, and I regret to say that it will not be in my power to accept your kind invitation, as I shall not be within striking distance of Philadelphia on the 20th.

Allow me to congratulate you on your brilliant and various successes, and Philadelphia for possessing such a citizen as yourself. The LEDGER, twenty years ago, when I lived in your city, was not a very good paper: the tone was rather low and hunkerish, and some of its articles excited in me great disgust. Perhaps, however, the fault was in me. The only fault I can find with the paper now is that your rates of advertising are too low; in other words, there is not enough reading in it. I doubt if any newspaper in the world ever came so near reaching the *whole* population of a city as yours does. Never have I known a house in Philadelphia that did not take the LEDGER. It is an awful power you wield, and I am glad to know that you are aware of the responsibility.

Very truly yours,

JAS. PARTON.

[From HENRY T. TUCKERMAN, Esq., the Essayist.]

NEW YORK, June 8, 1867.

Mr. Henry T. Tuckerman presents his compliments to Mr. George W. Childs, and begs leave to thank him for his kind invitation to unite in the festivities incident to the opening of the NEW LEDGER BUILDING, and to express his regret that circumstances will prevent him from availing himself of Mr. Childs' courtesy; and, at the same time, he desires to offer his congratulations to Mr. Childs on the success which has attended his liberal and honorable enterprise, and to express his best wishes for its continuance.

[From Henry C. Carey, LL. D., the well-known writer on Political Economy.]

Dear Sir: I shall be with you on Thursday, to aid in celebrating the triumph that, under your excellent management, the Ledger has achieved. Meantime, believe me, with great regard, Yours, faithfully,

G. W. Childs. HENRY C. CAREY.

Philadelphia, Monday, June 17.

[From Rev. Wm. R. Alger.]

Boston, June 5, 1867.

Mr. Geo. W. Childs.

My Dear Friend: A thousand thanks for your invitation to the great dinner at the "Continental," on the occasion of opening your New Ledger Building. A thousand hearty congratulations, also, on your prosperity. To see a good man prosper, is a sight of joy to all good men. I hope that in all things you may, for many a long year to come, flourish like a green bay tree.

Though not present at your noble feast in person, I shall be present in heart, and greet you with the high tribute of the hour. Ever, most cordially,

Your grateful friend,

WM. R. ALGER.

[From Rev. Henry Ward Beecher.]

Brooklyn, June 7, 1867.

Geo. W. Childs.

Dear Sir: It would give me very great pleasure to be in Philadelphia on the 20th, and to take part in the interesting festivities of that occasion. But I am tied hand and foot, and do not see that it will be possible for me to follow my promptings; and I shall be obliged to beg you to accept my good will, and to receive also my congratulations for your prosperity, and that of the Journal which you so ably manage. I am, very truly, yours,

H. W. BEECHER.

[From Epes Sargent, Esq., the Author.]

BOSTON, June 17, 1867.

MY DEAR MR. CHILDS: I regret that the prompt "I will come," with which I accepted your invitation, has to be followed by a "Pray, excuse me."

Obstacles I cannot well overcome will compel my absence. The loss will be mine, for I believe that almost all that there is of distinguished, in art and arms, literature and science, in the country, will be present (either in person or in spirit) at your munificent and unparalleled entertainment.

To me nothing conveys a more vivid idea of the immense growth of the country than the expansion of its newspaper establishments; and no success has been more striking, or more fairly earned, than that of the Philadelphia LEDGER. Never by a resort to questionable or illegitimate means of creating a sensation—never by lending itself to unworthy uses—never by lowering its moral tone, has it sought support. This is its great, its distinguishing merit, worthy of all commendation and all praise; and the superb building you have erected for your establishment is the fitting culmination of its renown; for it asserts, grandly and palpably, that even worldly success is compatible with a perfect uprightness unfounded on policy; thus contradicting that morbid Pyrrhonism of the day, which insinuates that in order to "succeed," one must not be over-nice in one's notions of honor, charity, and purity. Every great example of business success, attained without resort to charlatanism or chicane, or to any processes regarded as dubious by the moral sense, is better than a thousand sermons to our young men in favor of an upright career, pursued, not because it is *politic*, but because it is *upright*.

Such an example I believe to be yours, and so, my dear Mr. Childs, I wish you "God speed," and am

Yours, with sincere, constant regard,

GEO. W. CHILDS,   EPES SARGENT.
Philadelphia.

THE PUBLIC LEDGER BUILDING.

[From S. Austin Allibone, LL.D., author of the "Dictionary of Authors and Literature."]

1818 Spruce Street.
Philadelphia, June 26, 1867.

My Dear Mr. Childs: I was greatly interested in the ceremonies connected with the opening of the New Ledger Building, not the least feature of which was the grand banquet at the Continental Hotel, June 20th. It may be safely alleged, by any one conversant with the matter, that never were there gathered in one room in Philadelphia so many of her citizens (to say nothing of the eminent men from other portions of the country) distinguished in the various walks of science, literature, commerce, manufactures, mechanics, finance, and art; and on this assembly of notables, the military and naval chieftains conferred additional lustre. Looking back over the many years of our acquaintance, I naturally review the various excellent works which owe to you, in some cases, their birth—in all, a fostering care. How vividly I recall the adventurous and chivalric Kane, who, in the flush of his early manhood, with fond hearts at home, and brilliant prospects in the future, "counted not his life dear" unto himself, so that he might afford relief to, or bring back some tidings of, the lost navigators, or solve the great problem of the Arctic Sea! Well do I remember (sir, at that time, you and I were generally together a portion of each six days in the week) the zeal with which you personally superintended the preparation of his touching tale, and the liberality with which you, assuming all risks, awarded him a double copyright interest in his book, which paid to his representatives over sixty thousand dollars in about one year, and continued a source of profit for some time afterwards.

To the literature of Astronomy, History, and Law, you have been instrumental in adding the volumes of Bouvier, Sharswood, Brownlow, and Lossing—not to mention other volumes on which your tact and industry have also been conspicuous; and if I say nothing of the departments of literary biography, bibliography, and criticism, it is because I am unwilling, even upon an occasion like this, to be, in any respect, my own theme. The dedication page of my "Dictionary of Authors and Books," however, has not waited until this late day to make fitting acknowledgments to one of its best friends.

To return to your last and most important enterprise, the PUBLIC LEDGER, there was one point not adverted to at all by the speakers at the Continental banquet, probably for the satisfactory reason of its being unknown to them. From what was said respecting that excellent paper, the impression would be derived that you assumed the responsibility of its purchase at a time when one had nothing to do but to pocket the enormous revenue which it was, by its own action (as regular and unfailing as that of its admirable machinery), depositing daily on your counters. I, however, happened to know that you bought it (against the advice of almost every friend who conferred with you on the subject) at perhaps the darkest period of its history; when its losses were averaging about twelve thousand dollars per month. But you determined that it should "live and not die;" and you have now instilled into it a spirit of such vigorous activity, that it is likely long to live, the PEOPLE'S CYCLOPÆDIA OF USEFUL KNOWLEDGE.

With cordial wishes for your happiness and prosperity, I am, dear Mr. Childs,

Faithfully yours,

GEO. W. CHILDS.   S. AUSTIN ALLIBONE.

[From Rev. E. H. Chapin, D. D.]

NEW YORK, June 11, 1867.

GEO. W. CHILDS.

DEAR SIR: Accept my hearty congratulations at the well-earned success of the LEDGER, and my sincere wishes that its prosperity may continue and increase.

Yours, truly,

E. H. CHAPIN.

[From Rev. T. F. Curtis, D. D., late Professor in the University of Lewisburg, Pa.]

CAMBRIDGEPORT, MASS., June 12, 1867.

MY DEAR SIR: Your kind invitation to the opening of the NEW LEDGER BUILDING demands my best acknowledgments. Nothing intervening, I will certainly do myself the pleasure of accepting the invitation.

I regard the great success of the LEDGER enterprise as one of the most important triumphs of journalism in this or any other country, for it has been a success obtained through adherence to the most correct, liberal, and honorable principles. This is now the thirteenth year that I have been contributing to it, and it has been with a constantly increasing pleasure, for I feel that you have made it of the utmost value to the country.

Dr. Arnold, of Rugby, many years since, inspired me with the desire to write on public affairs, when I read of the solemn feeling with which that admirable man would peruse the daily journals as the chapter of providence appointed for him to study on that day. And my long knowledge of the traditionary principles by which the editorial rooms of the LEDGER office have been regulated, has made me increasingly in its power as a good agent for the community. There has always been that careful sifting out of fact from fiction and the prejudices with which party spirit has colored much that calls itself news.

When you assumed the proprietorship, I was delighted at the boldness with which you, at an enormous immediate cost, excluded every questionable advertisement; and by a new system of stereotyping, rendered the paper a welcome and indispensable guest in every family. The careful avoidance of all evil speaking and injurious personalities and scandals, I have ever known to be the settled policy, or rather principle of the LEDGER, one that has left it without enemies. Earnestly loyal throughout the war, it is no less conciliatory and reuniting to the whole country. Most impartial in its journalism, renowned for its enterprise in the earliest dissemination of facts, it inculcates well-ascertained truths without a superfluous word. Rising above party, it embraces heartily all that is true and permanent.

Its high and unexceptionable moral tone throughout has made it a good kind friend entering into nearly every house in the great City of Brotherly Love, and it has, without sect or party, sought to carry the principles of universal goodness and religion into each family.

To insure for a Journal conducted on such principles the brilliant, established, and permanent success that you have accomplished, is a triumph of Journalism of the highest moral significance and national importance.

Hoping that you may always be prospered in your further efforts for the public benefit,

Believe me, my dear sir,
Ever yours, most sincerely,
T. F. CURTIS.

[From Rev. M. Simpson, D. D., Bishop of the Methodist Episcopal Church.]

Philadelphia, June 19, 1867
Geo. W. Childs, Esq.

My Dear Sir: With great pleasure I accept your kind invitation to be present at the opening of the Ledger Building. I do so, because I highly appreciate the enterprise, taste, and skill you have manifested as well in the erection of a building of which the city will justly be proud, as in the editorial management of the Ledger since it has been under your supervision. But still more fully do I approve of the high moral tone which characterizes its pages. While as a newspaper its contents are rich and varied, no advertisements are admitted which foster immorality and vice. For the noble stand you have taken, you deserve the thanks of every family circle, and of all good citizens. From the depths of my heart, I wish you great success,   And with high regard
I am, yours truly,
M. SIMPSON.

THE PUBLIC LEDGER BUILDING.

[From Rev. C. P. Krauth, D. D., Norton Professor of Theology in the Theological Seminary of the Evangelical Lutheran Church in Philadelphia.]

Philadelphia, June 16, 1867.

My Dear Mr. Childs: My absence from the city will prevent my acceptance of your kind invitation to be present at the opening of the Ledger Building and at the dinner which is to follow it. I do not claim the character of a prophet, and know that I run no risk of proving myself a false one, in predicting that the arrangements will be princely, and worthy of your reputation for munificence and good taste.

In the ever-widening circle of your friends, among whom it is my privilege to have been one of the earliest, I am sure you have none who with a deeper interest and admiration than mine have watched your growing prosperity. I have rejoiced to see it so brilliant, yet so solid. You have conjoined the rapidity which shows your genius as a man of business, with the stability which is the result of sobriety, of judgment, and indefatigable industry. You have united the active imagination which originates great plans, with the mathematical exactness which accurately marks their necessary details, and the practical skill which consummates them.

You have made the literary and scientific world your debtor by publishing some of the best books of this century in a style worthy of the names of Allibone, Kane, Bouvier, Kidder, Peterson, Sheppard, and Sharswood. You took the Ledger, and have given it a hold upon the relatively fastidious few, without weakening its influence or popularity with the masses. It has become more instructive, without becoming less reliable. You have rendered it more than ever a mirror of the living world, but you have shown your determination that the breath of impurity shall never sully it. You have made the Ledger a great power, and all good men thank you that its influence is exercised in the interests of truth and of pure morals. It is as careful to sift intelligence as it is enterprising to collect it; and because it knows that nothing is really new that is not really true, it is at once soonest and safest in its chronicle of the day. Its advertising columns are in themselves a marvellous record of what the thousands have or want, and furnish a silent exchange whose value and absolute necessity the whole community comes gradually, by personal experience, to understand. You have prospered as have those few men who excite the envy of their kind, but your success has been so fairly won, so richly merited, so generously shared with others, so freely used to aid in all good works, and you have been so courteous and just in all your relations, that envy itself has been disarmed.

That you may long live to enjoy the blessings with which a gracious Providence has crowned your enterprise and labor, and that in the memory of one world, and in the rewards of another, you may take a place with the benefactors of mankind, is the very hearty wish of

Your friend,
C. P. KRAUTH.

[From Rev. J. P. Thompson, D. D., Pastor of Tabernacle Church, N. Y. City.]

NEW YORK, June 5, 1867.

MR. GEO. W. CHILDS.

MY DEAR SIR: Most heartily do I thank you for the invitation to the inauguration of the LEDGER in its new building. I should delight in meeting such a circle of literary and professional gentlemen as your hospitality will bring together, and in rendering my own humble tribute to your eminent services to the press and the literature of our country. But your festive-day will be the annual gala-day of my Sunday school, and I must forego my own pleasure that I may contribute to that of children.

With high regard,
Truly yours,
JOS. P. THOMPSON.

THE PUBLIC LEDGER BUILDING.

[From Hon. EMORY WASHBURN, LL. D., Ex-Governor of Massachusetts, and Resident Prof. of Law at Harvard University.]

CAMBRIDGE, MASS., June 28, 1867.

GEO. W. CHILDS, ESQ.

DEAR SIR: Your card of invitation for the opening of the NEW LEDGER BUILDING on the 20th inst., for which I ought earlier to have thanked you, came duly to hand, and awakened a strong desire on my part to avail myself of the pleasure which the occasion was sure to afford; but a domestic event, occurring on the same day, precluded the *possibility* of my being present, and a variety of pressing engagements have prevented my earlier expressing the regret I felt at losing the interesting ceremonies and eloquent remarks of the occasion. As it is, I can only say I thank you for having included me in the number of those whom you honored by remembering in connection with that event.

The press has appropriately noticed the occasion, but it has by no means exaggerated its interest or importance. To you it must have been a day of conscious pride and satisfaction, as it bore testimony to the position you hold in the conduct of that power of the press which is stronger than any other single power in the nation.

Few men, I apprehend, are aware of the responsibility of a manager of a leading newspaper in our country, where everybody reads, and so many borrow the tone and character of their opinions from what emanates from the press. It has grown to be the medium through which the public thought is reached and controlled. I am struck with awe when I think of the amount of good or evil, of truth or error, which goes out into the community with every issue of such a paper as the LEDGER. It finds its way into the homes of the rich and poor, into the shop of the artisan, and the offices and counting-rooms of men of trade and business, and silently works its way into the confidence and conviction of its readers. People are coming to appreciate this element of power more and more every year,

The daily and weekly press is no longer the organ of political success alone, but is called in to the aid of every scheme or system that involves the co-operation of numbers, whether it be religion, benevolence, or social or political economy. Now, I repeat, to be one of the comparatively few who wield this power is a position of influence and importance which can hardly be exaggerated.

I have no doubt you will worthily sustain the place which you had already won, and which the opening of the NEW LEDGER BUILDING has confirmed, in your new relation to the public press. And it would have given me great pleasure to join in the congregation of your friends on that auspicious occasion. What you have done will become historic hereafter. The beautiful temple of Art which you have reared as a monument of your own taste and enterprise, will, I doubt not, hereafter be the home of taste, culture, and good sense; which, in these practical days of ours, are far better adapted to the condition of the times than the Muses of which we read in classic story.

I trust I may, some time, have the pleasure to see for myself what I now know only from description; and perhaps catch a lingering echo of that eloquence to which its dedication gave utterance. I shall trust to finding you still its presiding genius, and to renew the assurance that I now offer, that I am

Yours, truly and respectfully,
EMORY WASHBURN.

[From HENRY COPPÉE, LL.D., President of the Lehigh University, Pa.]

BETHLEHEM, PA., June 11, 1867.

MY DEAR MR. CHILDS: All prosperity to the LEDGER, and to its excellent and distinguished proprietor, is the wish of his sincere friend,

HENRY COPPEE.

[From Professor C. W. Shields, D.D.]

PRINCETON COLLEGE, N. J., June 14, 1867.

MY DEAR MR. CHILDS: The opening of the NEW LEDGER BUILDING will bring to public view the fact that a daily newspaper of sound moral tone, free from abusive personalities or sensational appeals, and the organ of no mere sect or party, is liberally sustained by the whole people; and, moreover, that such a paper can be made to embrace, together with all the various industrial interests of the community, whatever is of practical value in science or literature.

The temptations to a different style of journalism in our day are very great; but I know that it has been the noble ambition of your life to become a public benefactor as well as a successful journalist, and the high position you have reached is but the just reward of principles to which you have adhered through all your course.

I anticipate for the LEDGER an increasing influence among all classes. Your field of operations will now be greatly enlarged, and with such a firm hold of popular confidence, you will be able to educate, as well as reflect, a sound *public* sentiment in every department of life, and upon all questions.

As one of your oldest friends, I have confidently looked forward to your success, and now rejoice in it with a peculiar pride and pleasure.

With sincere regard,
Faithfully yours,
CHARLES W. SHIELDS.

GEORGE W. CHILDS.

CORRESPONDENCE.

[From M. L. Stoever, Professor in Pennsylvania College.]

GETTYSBURG, June 12, 1867.

MY WORTHY FRIEND: I am sorry my official duties will prevent me from being with you on so interesting an occasion as the dedication of your building. I shall be with you in spirit, although absent in the body. I rejoice in the success which has crowned your past labors. Your remarkable career is a beautiful illustration of the influence of American institutions.

I am, as ever, faithfully,
Your friend,
M. L. STOEVER.

[From Hon. John H. D. Latrobe.]

BALTIMORE, June 26, 1867.

MY DEAR MR. CHILDS: Had your invitation not been mislaid, I would have made it a point to be present on the occasion, to testify my appreciation of the energy and talent of which the New Building is an evidence, as well as my esteem for my host personally. Again expressing my regret, I am most truly yours,
JNO. H. D. LATROBE.

[From Dr. Hammond, late Surgeon-General of the U. S. Army.]

NEW YORK, June 12, 1867.

MY DEAR SIR: I have delayed responding to your kind invitation, hoping that I might be able to accept it. I find, however, that it will be impossible for me to do so. I trust you will have a successful inauguration of your elegant building, and that you will long continue at the head of the great enterprise you have so energetically conducted.

With great regard,
I am yours sincerely,
WILLIAM A. HAMMOND.

GEORGE W. CHILDS, Esq., Philadelphia.

[From Geo. H. Boker, Esq., Secretary of the Union League of Philadelphia.]

PHILADELPHIA, June 13, 1867.

MY DEAR SIR: It will afford me great pleasure to be present at the ceremonies that will attend the opening of the NEW LEDGER BUILDING on the 20th of this month, and to give my humble countenance to the deserved public honors that will then doubtless be paid to you and to your newspaper.

I have more than once expressed to you my high estimate of the patriotic course of the LEDGER during the late war of the rebellion, and of the valuable services which your newspaper rendered to the national cause by the high tone which characterized its editorials during the most disheartening periods of the great struggle. This support had the greater influence with the people, because the LEDGER was not known as a partisan newspaper, nor as the advocate of any political creed; and circulating as it did, in the widest manner, amongst all classes of the people, its broad and vigorous national views must have carried great weight and convincing power into the minds of the popular masses. I know of no one newspaper that was more useful for good in those dark days of our history than that which you now control. In these times of peace and returning prosperity, the remembrance of what your newspaper accomplished for the country, in her hour of need, must be a pleasant reflection for you, amidst your new labors. Added to that, I hear on all sides warm commendations bestowed upon you, for the many admirable changes which you have made in the LEDGER since it came into your hands, and for the fresh spirit which you have given to its columns, as well as of the increasing prosperity of its business. No better evidence of that prosperity can be called for, than the sight of the noble building which you have erected for your purposes; and I feel assured that the banquet with which you propose to open your spacious printing-house will be a memorable event in the annals of American newspapers.

With such a history and such prospects, you will feel no doubt of the fair fortune that is in store for the LEDGER, which no one will hail with more pleasure than

     Your obedient servant,
        GEO. H. BOKER.

GEO. W. CHILDS, ESQ.

[From the Hon. GEO. W. WOODWARD, LL D., Chief-Justice of the Supreme Court of Pennsylvania.]

     WILKESBARRE, June 4, 1867.

GEO. W. CHILDS.

DEAR SIR: You may be assured of the great pleasure with which I have observed your enterprising arrangements for the future, and of my sincere hope that you may realize the rich reward you so well deserve.

  I am, dear sir, very truly,
    Your obedient servant,
       GEO. W. WOODWARD.

[From the Hon. GEORGE SHARSWOOD, LL. D., President Judge of the District Court of Philadelphia.]

     JUNE 12, 1867.

MY DEAR MR. CHILDS: I shall not be able to accept your polite invitation to the opening of the LEDGER BUILDING on Thursday, June 20, and to dinner. It would give me great pleasure to be with you, but you can see it would be awkward, if not improper, for a candidate for a judicial office to appear on what would be a public or *quasi* public occasion. I hope you may have a very merry time, and that it may inaugurate to you a course of increased prosperity and usefulness.

    Yours, very truly,
       GEO. SHARSWOOD.

THE PUBLIC LEDGER BUILDING.

[From J. I. CLARK HARE, Associate Justice of the District Court of Philadelphia.]

DEAR SIR: Thanks to your hospitality I passed on Thursday last a most agreeable evening, and my pleasure was certainly not less because the number of guests from other States rendered it fitting that some of us who were nearer home should be silent. If the occasion had arisen, I should have been happy to respond to any call that might have been made upon me by the LEDGER on behalf of the press, and my chief difficulty in complying with your request that I should write what I might have said is a doubt whether the thoughts that occurred to me merit publication. I wish, however to express my sense of the importance of every onward movement of the journals that have so large an influence in shaping the future of this country and of civilization, and to say how significant it seemed to me to be of the spirit of the age, that if the costly structure which we were inaugurating might justly be termed palatial, it was a palace destined to be the abode of industry, and of that industry which most elevates and refines mankind—the industry of the printer. The rest of the world owes much to him, and we in this country shall never be able to compute the magnitude of our debt. The trite maxim that in a popular government everything depends on the virtue and intelligence of the people, is now for the first time in the full sense true, because never until now has government been intrusted without check or qualification to universal suffrage.

That we are not worse than men have been in other times and countries is not a sufficient answer to criticism; we must be much better if we would escape the fate which has hitherto attended the efforts of mankind for freedom. Our political task is the greatest and most difficult that has yet been essayed, and cannot be accomplished without raising the many to a moral and political height that has hitherto been reserved for the privileged few. For this purpose the daily press is a powerful instrument, more effectual in some respects even than the pulpit and the public school. The newspaper is the library of the poor man; nor his alone, but that of the numerous class which, having ample means to buy books, wants the leisure or inclination to read them. For the changes of politics, the result of campaigns, the fall or foundation of States and kingdoms—for all, in fine, that makes up the sum of cotemporary history, we look to its pages; but they also contain a fund of information on other topics, past and present, so varied and extensive, that few men who have not considered the subject are aware how much they would lose if all that they have learned from that source were erased from their memories. We might, therefore, well unite with the eloquent divine who said grace before the entertainment, in thanking God for "printing and the power of the press"—as the power having the greatest capacity for good, with the least tendency to evil. A statesman of the last generation declared his willingness to let others make the laws if he might write the ballads of his country; but the ballad has, in these United States, been replaced by the leading article; and he who would know what form legislation will take in the coming years must look to the ideas inculcated by the press of to-day. Whatever, therefore, tends to chasten and exalt the influence of the daily press merits the attention of every one who cares either for the public good or his individual interest, and it was this which, even more than numbers and brilliancy, gave significance to the celebration of the other day. All who adverted to the subject on that occasion agreed that the success which the LEDGER achieved almost from the outset was due to its having supplied a public need, which may be illustrated by a reference to my own profession. The struggle which is constantly going on before the tribunal of public opinion between the great political parties has an analogy to that occurring between rival litigants in a court of justice. The country is the jury, and the journals on either side appear as advocates. Their end is truth, the maintenance of great ideas and principles; but the truths which they especially affect are apt to predominate over others that are not for the time being so much in vogue. Less than this would not answer the purpose, which is, to array all the facts and reasons in favor of a particular line of policy, leaving the argument against it to be made by its opponents. And no one who considers the matter fairly can doubt that such advocacy is in the actual state of things as essential to the conduct of public affairs, as the energy and devotion of the lawyer are to the full and thorough investigation of the cause of his client. But there will, notwithstanding, as society advances, be a growing demand for newspapers whose columns shall be open to the entrance of truth in every form, without regard to the question whence it comes, or the effect that it may have on preconceived opinions. Such a journal would occupy the position of an arbiter moderating the spirit of party, schooling the faults of public men, and tending, as far as the diversity of human nature permits, to bring mankind to a common ground of sense and virtue. And if I am right in my conjecture, some part, at least, of the success that attended the LEDGER is due to its having been among the first to occupy a field that will hereafter be found susceptible of even greater usefulness. Yours, truly,

J. I. CLARK HARE.

PHILADELPHIA, Wednesday, July 3, 1867.
GEORGE W. CHILDS, ESQ.

[From JOSEPH HARRISON, M. E.]

PHILADELPHIA, June 19, 1867.

MR. GEO. W. CHILDS.

MY DEAR FRIEND: The erection of such a pile as the LEDGER BUILDING is an event in our city. Its success, and the success of the LEDGER, are assured. May you long live to fill the place you now occupy in our community; and to enjoy the honors you have earned and so well deserve is the sincere wish of Yours, most truly,

JOSEPH HARRISON.

[From Geo. S. Appleton, Esq. (D. Appleton & Co., Publishers), New York.]

New York, June 16, 1867.

My Dear Mr. Childs: I congratulate you on having completed the edifice which, from all accounts, is the finest, as well as the largest, newspaper office in the United States.

I do not know that it is possible for you to print any more than you do now, but I have no doubt that this exhibition of extraordinary enterprise will increase your circulation.

When the great ledger of life, where all our deeds and actions are recorded, shall be opened, I think that the record of the Ledger, under your administration, will stand higher, for purity of expression and freedom from slander of personal character, than any paper I know of. The responsibility of a public journal, with its million of readers, is immense. The obscure and humble individual, who never writes for the press, can only poison his own mind; whilst the public journalist may be the means of poisoning the minds of thousands.

May God prosper you!

Very truly yours,
GEO. S. APPLETON.

[From W. B. Dinsmore, President of the Adams Express Company.]

Stratsburg, N. Y.

My Dear Sir: I wish you all sorts of success in the enterprise on which you have embarked, and which has so wonderfully prospered under your hands. May you continue to grow rich, until, satiated with legal tenders, you wend your way to the banks of the Hudson, and pass the remainder of your days beneath the shadows of her lofty trees, and among the good and virtuous of her people!

With great respect,
I remain your obedient servant,
W. B. DINSMORE.

Geo. W. Childs, Esq.

THE PUBLIC LEDGER BUILDING.

[From Col. R. M. Hoe, Inventor of Hoe's celebrated Printing Presses.]

NEW YORK, June 24, 1867.

MY DEAR MR. CHILDS: As I telegraphed you, I regretted very much that I was compelled to forego the pleasure of being present at your opening of the NEW LEDGER BUILDING, as I had fully intended to be. Every advance in the usefulness and prosperity of the LEDGER cannot fail to interest me, and I would have liked very much indeed to join with your many friends in wishing success to the LEDGER and its present proprietor and manager. What should be the duration of a public newspaper, the world is not yet old enough to tell; but if one may judge of a tree by its fruits, the LEDGER, for all I can see, is likely to be perennial. At any rate, in its present hands, it will lack for nothing. I well remember the patient industry and firm resolve which characterized the establishment of the LEDGER, to make it in all respects a perfectly reliable newspaper, and on all subjects to consider the public welfare, treating all subjects and persons simply upon merit; always aiming to express, on important national events and topics, the best sense of the American people. I have been familiar with its whole history during the thirty-one years of its existence, and was very intimate with its former proprietors, especially with my old friend, Mr. Swain, whom I always regarded as one of the soundest thinkers connected with the newspaper press. I know it was his and his partners', Messrs. Abell and Simmons, constant study and aim to give the LEDGER a sterling character and individuality of its own, lifting it far above all party or personal influences, and, regarding only the public welfare, associated the best talent in its editorials and conduct—the LEDGER alone responsible, the writers always anonymous. His (Mr. Swain's) sound views, and steadfastness in maintaining them, and able financial management, established the LEDGER on a most enviable and durable basis. These facts are well known to you, and no doubt induced you to become its proprietor.

I am certain that the many improvements you are making are but the legitimate growth of the paper in your hands, and doubt not that the resources, energy, and ability you are so bountifully bestowing upon it will increase its usefulness, power, and prominence.

There is no position in life, it has always seemed to me, more ennobling than that of a conductor of a well-established and prominent public journal—none that gives opportunity for greater usefulness, nor one that involves more grave responsibility.

I trust you may live long to enjoy the high position acquired by your own ability and industry.

     Yours, very truly,
        RICHARD M. HOE.

Geo. W. Childs,
  Philadelphia.

[From R. Dunglison, M. D., Professor in the Jefferson Medical College. Philadelphia.]

    1110 Girard St., Philadelphia, June 17, 1867.

Geo. W. Childs, Esq.

My Dear Sir: Most reluctantly am I compelled to decline your kind invitation to be present at the opening of your magnificent establishment on Thursday next. My impaired physical condition has constrained me to relinquish this and numerous other social enjoyments. I beg of you to accept my warm acknowledgments for your goodness on this as well as on former occasions, and my cordial wishes for a continuance of that prosperity which has hitherto resulted from your well-devised and well-directed endeavors for the diffusion of knowledge.

    I am, very dear sir,
     Very truly yours,
       ROBLEY DUNGLISON.

THE PUBLIC LEDGER BUILDING.

(From General E. S. SANFORD, late President of the American Telegraph Company.)

NEW YORK, June 13, 1867.

MY DEAR FRIEND: It gives me great pleasure to accept your kind invitation to help celebrate the opening of the NEW LEDGER BUILDING, and afterwards dine with a part of your friends at the Continental Hotel.

I cannot quite say that I have been familiar with the LEDGER from its start, but I have had very close and pleasant relations with its owners and managers from 1843 to the present date. I learned many lessons for the conducting of my own business from the clear-headed, persevering, and strongly-determined men who wielded its power until 1864.

The purchase by you was a surprise to me; but one of my first reflections upon the change was, "This will show the wisdom of the late proprietors, who always strove to make the paper represent, not them, but itself." It was not somebody's newspaper, it was always the LEDGER; and when it had grown into a power, was capable of being transferred an unimpaired power.

Although my acquaintance with you (which, I trust, has ripened into friendship) began at a much later date than with the LEDGER, you had made sufficient mark to convince me you were equal to showing what the LEDGER could become, especially when aided by your associate, Mr. A. J. Drexel, whom I have known from the time he was a lad, and honored for his straightforwardness, liberality, and great ability since manhood has developed his character.

Trusting that you may have a continuance of that success, which I am sure you will merit,

I am yours, truly,
EDWARDS S. SANFORD.

GEO. W. CHILDS, Esq.

[From HARPER & BROTHERS, Publishers, New York.]

NEW YORK, June 14, 1867.

DEAR MR. CHILDS: We beg you to accept our acknowledgments for the invitation with which you have favored us to be present at the inauguration of the NEW LEDGER BUILDING on the 20th inst.

The "Brothers" who now write have been for well nigh half a century "Brothers of the Craft," and no ordinary obstacle would prevent them from being present in the city of "Brotherly Love" on an occasion where they would be sure to meet so many of their old friends and new associates.

But it so happens that of us four one is now in Europe, and he could only arrive in time by way of the Atlantic Telegraph, which, we believe, does not yet carry messages of his weight.

Another of us comes near having the excuse found valid in Holy Writ, on an occasion somewhat similar. He has not exactly just "married a wife," and therefore prays that you "will have him excused;" but on that day the wedding of his daughter is to take place, and the bride elect properly insists that for this one occasion her claims upon her father and upon her father's brothers shall take precedence of everything else.

We pray you to accept our warmest congratulations upon the completion of your magnificent structure, and our most sincere wishes for your continued prosperity and happiness.

You have richly earned, by your persevering industry and enlightened enterprise, the decided success which you have so happily achieved. May it be long continued, and even increased tenfold, and eventually prove a rich inheritance to your children's children!

Very faithfully yours,
HARPER & BROTHERS.

[From John Walter, Esq., M. P., Proprietor of the "London Times."]

40 Upper Grosvenor Street,
London, England, July 11, 1867.

My Dear Sir: I received with great pleasure a copy of the pamphlet containing an account of your new establishment. I beg to offer you my hearty congratulations on the successful completion of your vast undertaking, which I trust will be the means of adding to the circulation and prosperity of the LEDGER.

With kindest regards to Mrs. Childs, I remain

Yours, very truly,
J. WALTER.

[From J. T. Fields, Esq. (Ticknor & Fields, Publishers), Boston.]

Boston, June 5, 1867.

My Dear Childs: I wish it were in my power to be with you and your guests on the happy occasion to which you so kindly invite me. You will have a grand time, and I would gladly join in it, for I know the excellent ability of Philadelphia to accomplish all that is best in the way of hospitality and good cheer. If I could possibly attend your festival, you know I would do so; but I have an engagement, made years ago, to spend all my months of June in New Hampshire, my native State, and I can't break it now. Take, then, all my best wishes, dear friend, for your continued success. The LEDGER is a capital paper: make it better still, if possible. Its circulation is among the largest in the world: beat them all during the coming year. The proprietor is an enterprising young man—and here I stop wishing, and beg to remain, always,

Yours, most sincerely,
JAMES T. FIELDS.

CORRESPONDENCE.

[From THEODORE TILTON, Esq., Editor of "The Independent."]

NEW YORK, June 14, 1867.

MY DEAR MR. CHILDS: At the time of your feast I shall be a thousand miles from Philadelphia; "I pray thee, therefore, have me excused." But, though absent from a seat at the table, let me rejoice with a newspaper that is able to "eat, drink, and be merry." I trust that the starvation period for newspapers and their editors is gone, never to return. I congratulate you on your prosperity, both physical and pecuniary! May your shadow never be less! Ever yours,

THEODORE TILTON.

[From Rev. WM. M. ENGLES, D. D., Editor of "The Presbyterian."]

PHILADELPHIA, June 13, 1867.

MY DEAR MR. CHILDS: I thank you for your kind invitation to be present at the inauguration of your new and elegant structure, but from a long withdrawal from all participation in public demonstrations, I feel myself to be wholly unadapted to grace by my presence so distinguished an occasion.

My interest in you personally, if anything could, would induce me to overcome my reluctance and timidity in this instance; but my secluded habits have become so chronic as to be invincible.

I appreciate so highly your public spirit and generosity, and am so impressed with the political fairness and conservative moral tone of the PUBLIC LEDGER, under your management, that you have my cordial good wishes for success in every useful enterprise. For about thirty-three years I have been the editor of a religious journal, "The Presbyterian," and hence feel much interest in every attempt to elevate the character of secular journalism.

With most friendly consideration,
I remain yours, truly,

WM. M. ENGLES.

[From GEO. P. PUTNAM, Esq., Publisher, New York.]

NEW YORK, June 12, 1867.

MY DEAR CHILDS: Your card asks for a response— Won't I be there? Most assuredly, Providence permitting. No light matter will keep me away.

For why? Not merely because I want to see your splendid new establishment, the fame of which has already gone abroad, nor because I know that, with your accustomed hospitality, you will generously entertain your guests, but because I shall be one of the hundreds of personal friends who will delight in the opportunity of joining in the tributes of personal regard to yourself, and warm congratulations on this last great landmark of your prosperous career and your well-deserved success.

As a publisher of books, if you had achieved no other successes than those connected with the names of Kane, Bouvier, and Allibone, your name would remain embalmed for posterity; and we of "the trade" all know that in those and other enterprises you have shown a liberal sagacity, taste, and enterprise rare in our fraternity. That you should also accomplish a notable advancement in the business machinery and the profitable results of a daily newspaper was a perfectly logical sequence. Such an enterprise as would positively frighten most of us timid and slow-moving old fogies, you, in your shrewd energy and wide-awake sagacity, enter upon as a pastime. You wave your magic wand, and lo! palaces rise, and the genii of steam and lightning send forth from their subterranean cells and lofty attics tens of thousands of daily messages over the continent; and fortune follows deservedly, because you regulate all these powers on liberal principles of justice and truth.

But I really did not mean to write rounded periods of fulsome eulogy, but only to express—what I may have no chance to do on the great occasion—my honest admiration of your sagacious progress and your merited success; and to join your hosts of friends in heartily wishing you continued prosperity, fame, and profit in the responsible and important position of controller of a leading daily newspaper.

If any of your friends may be more emphatic than others in cordial good wishes on this occasion, it is *I*, whom you have always treated in such a truly friendly and brotherly spirit, crowning many lesser acts of disinterested generosity with that important and substantial one when you so promptly and cheerfully gave your name for large responsibility in guaranteeing the good faith of your brother publisher, sinking, alas! from that proud position to the meaner office of—publican! From this last, thanks to the politicians, I am now happily released, and you, my worthy friend, will be relieved from the danger you so generously braved, of having to pay over any portion of that $100,000 you guaranteed to our "mutual uncle." Let us congratulate each other! And should you ever, in the course of human events, be a candidate for the Presidency, or for the office of tax-gatherer, it will be a hard case if you don't find sponsors ready to imitate, although they may not excel, the unselfish magnanimity and benevolence of "G. W. C."

Accept my earnest wishes for the continued prosperity of your great enterprises, and your own personal health, happiness, and usefulness as a discriminating benefactor of the City of Brotherly Love.

Your obliged friend,
G. P. PUTNAM.

[From Dr. J. G. HOLLAND (Timothy Titcomb), the well-known author.]

SPRINGFIELD, MASS., June 10, 1867.

GEO. W. CHILDS, ESQ.

MY DEAR SIR: Though it will not be practicable for me to accept your polite invitation to the banquet, by which you propose to celebrate the completion of your NEW LEDGER BUILDING, I cannot refrain from sending to you my congratulations on your achievement, and the business success of which it is, at once, the product and the monument. I know something of what success in a newspaper enterprise means; I know something of what such a success costs. I was for many years connected with a newspaper, as you know; and I know, as none but an editor can know, what the indispensable elements of success are. An author may win a name by a single book that may have cost him no more than a year of labor. An orator, inspired by some great occasion, may achieve renown by one brilliant effort, and carry the laurels green and fresh for many years. A speculator, by a lucky turn in the market, may, in one bold dash, find himself the possessor of an unearned million. But the conductor of a newspaper cannot hope to achieve his success by a single number, or by a year of excellence. Day after day, week after week, month after month, year after year, decade after decade, he must work, work, work. Not a day of effort can be missed. He must be always fresh, piquant, thorough, industrious, and alive. To him repose never comes. He must see everything, hear everything, know everything, record everything. He must have a quick insight into the people's wants, and supply it unwearyingly.

So, whenever I witness a great success in newspaper enterprise, I know it is the reward of faithful work. I know that success in this business is only won by work; and this new building of yours is your diploma. It is a monument of well-directed, faithful, and long-continued industry. It is the summing-up of a long and worthy history. It is the fruit of a tree that was well planted at the first, and that has been pruned, watered, fertilized, trained, and tended by patient and careful hands, through all the days of many years. It is the representation, in stone and mortar, of blood, vitality, and brains, expended under the direction of the virtues of patience and industry.

Knowing, therefore, that this new building has not a stone in it, that was not worthily earned, I give you my congratulations. May the blessing of God rest upon it, and upon the man who directs its enterprises, and may the future of the LEDGER be as useful, as brilliant, and as successful as its past has been! I do not know that I have any better wish for you, unless it be that you may visit me, and learn how comfortable an old editor can be when divested of his harness and turned out to grass.

Yours, very truly,
J. G. HOLLAND.

[From Rev. Dr. CROOKS, Editor of "The Methodist."]

OFFICE OF "THE METHODIST,"
NEW YORK, June 10, 1867.

GEO. W. CHILDS.

MY DEAR SIR: I greatly regret that my engagements will not permit me to be present at the opening of the NEW LEDGER BUILDING to the public. Allow me, however, to offer you my congratulations upon your success as the conductor of a daily paper. Your effort to raise the tone of journalism was hailed with satisfaction by all who feel the importance of social morality, and has been, I am glad to say, generously sustained by the public.

I well remember the early history of the PUBLIC LEDGER. It was a diminutive sheet, and along side of the "United States Gazette," so long edited by the scholarly Chandler, it looked too small to aspire to rivalry. It found a home at once among the masses, who have ever since stood by it. Long may it prosper! Yours, sincerely,

G. R. CROOKS.

THE PUBLIC LEDGER BUILDING.

[From Col. Greene, Editor of the "Boston Post."]

Office of the "Boston Post,"
Boston, 15th June, 1867.

My Dear Mr. Childs: It would afford me much gratification to be present at the dedication of the grand monument to your enterprise and ability as a publisher, if it were in my power; but engagements confine me here. I assure you, however, none will witness the ceremony with more satisfaction than your humble servant, who has devoted himself for nearly half a century to the business you have so honorably distinguished. Mr. Gladstone truly spoke when he said the newspaper press was interwoven with the whole tissue of modern life, and that you cannot tear it out; and if you could, that tissue would be rent into shreds, so as to lose all signs of its identity. Bearing this important relation to society, gentlemen who direct the press exercise great power for evil, and those like yourself, who find their labors in this sphere sanctioned by the cordial approbation and liberal support of a great, moral, and intelligent community, are entitled to the reward due to good and faithful servants; and that such reward may be yours here and hereafter, is the prayer of

Your friend,
C. G. GREENE.

[From E. P. Whipple, Esq.]

"Evening Transcript" Office,
Boston, June 5, 1867.

My Dear Mr. Childs: I regret very much my inability to be present at your grand "Opening." It must be a great occasion for you and the Ledger, and I would that I could be there to see; but my engagements here will prevent my having that pleasure.

With best wishes for your success in all things,
I remain, very truly, yours,
E. P. WHIPPLE.

CORRESPONDENCE.

[From the Editors and Proprietors of the "Journal of Commerce,"
New York.]

OFFICE OF THE "JOURNAL OF COMMERCE,"
NEW YORK, June 11, 1867.

MR. GEO. W. CHILDS.

DEAR SIR: I congratulate you and the LEDGER on the prosperity which calls for a new building, and were I addressing the public, I would congratulate them upon having in their service an "Institution" at once so conservative and so active as the enterprising establishment whose fortunes you represent.

I regret that I cannot share in your festivities on the 20th inst. I have not been away from this office two week-days in succession (except over a national holiday), for eighteen years, and I have become a rusted fixture, nearly immovable.

Wishing you all that success you so richly deserve, and thanking you for your kind invitation, I am

Your friend and obedient servant,
DAVID M. STONE.

OFFICE OF THE "JOURNAL OF COMMERCE,"
NEW YORK, June 4, 1867.

GEO. W. CHILDS.

MY DEAR SIR: With the most sincere good wishes for your prosperity and that of the LEDGER,

I am truly yours,
W. C. PRIME.

[From F. B. PENNIMAN, Esq., Editor of the "Pittsburgh Gazette."]

OFFICE OF THE "GAZETTE,"
PITTSBURGH, June 4, 1867.

MR. GEO. W. CHILDS.

DEAR SIR: As a fellow townsman and fellow apprentice with the founder of the LEDGER, and a sincere admirer of the tact and talent with which it has ever been managed, by him and by you, it would afford me great pleasure to be present on that occasion.   Very truly yours,

F. B. PENNIMAN.

THE PUBLIC LEDGER BUILDING.

[From M. HALSTEAD, Esq., Editor and Proprietor of the "Cincinnati Commercial."]

OFFICE OF THE "CINCINNATI COMMERCIAL,"
CINCINNATI, June 5, 1867.

GEO. W. CHILDS.

DEAR SIR: If I could, I would be with you at the formal opening of the NEW LEDGER BUILDING on the 20th. It is an incident in the progress of journalism in which I feel an especial interest. I hope you have built the "model newspaper office" in the country. I will take great satisfaction, whenever I visit your city, in inspecting it. Having been engaged for nearly twenty years in the newspaper business, you may infer that I have accumulated some views on the subject of the construction of newspaper offices. As to newspaper management, the LEDGER (yours, not Bonner's) is and has long been a favorite of mine, as I have an especial admiration for a truly and thoroughly independent newspaper; a paper that is conducted for the express purpose of placing before the public intelligence of general interest, without any partisan or sectarian bias or coloring; the publication of facts, irrespective of whom they may help or hurt.

But the feature of the LEDGER that commends itself to me most decidedly is that of making a rigorous distinction between advertisements and reading-matter. I read with especial pleasure recently, in the proceedings of the District Court of your city, the testimony that in the LEDGER "no paid matter was allowed to appear in the local or editorial columns." I can say to you that, after a long struggle, we have definitely established that rule in the management of the "Commercial;" that no paid matter, under any circumstances, appears in the paper, except under the regular classification heads of the advertising departments. I consider that an essential feature of an independent journal, and one the general establishment of which is necessary to insure the self-respect of journalists and to make the newspaper business legitimate and honorable.

Looking over your personal history in a recent copy of the "Chimney Corner," I find that you were born in the same year with myself; that you are described as " of sanguine temperament, ruddy complexion, fresh and decidedly healthful appearance." All that, I suppose, I may claim for myself. In your portrait in the "Chimney Corner" I observe that there is a scarcity of the capillary adornment of the cranium. I can offset that by prematurely gray whiskers; but I am not an owner of the fine, open, and pleasing expression of the countenance, or of that which is said in compliment of your manners.

If the editorial corps of the "Commercial" were not reduced to the minimum, by the absence of members at the Paris Exposition and the Rocky Mountain Buffalo Hunt, I would certainly accept your kind invitation, and be present at the formal opening. As it is, I must content myself with this expression of kind wishes.

Very truly yours,

M. HALSTEAD.

[From JOSHUA LEAVITT, Esq.]

OFFICE OF THE "EVENING POST,"
NEW YORK, June 11, 1867.

MR. GEO. W. CHILDS.

DEAR SIR: It would give me great pleasure to join the company who will congratulate the LEDGER and its proprietor in its occupancy of the new building which so fitly honors its enterprise and crowns its success. The power of an honest and patriotic press to subsist and triumph, as the champion of public morals and justice, without the support of party or sect, is a pregnant fact to illustrate the inner life of this republic, and inspires unlimited confidence in the perpetuity of the institutions under whose shadow such plants live and thrive.

Wishing you the continuance and increase of success with the increase of effort,

I remain, with much respect, your friend,

JOSHUA LEAVITT.

[From R. Shelton Mackenzie, D.C.L.]

Office of "The Press,"
Philadelphia, June 14, 1867.

My Dear Mr. Childs: I feel honored as well as gratified by your invitation to assist at the opening of the Ledger New Building, and cordially accept it.

Perhaps I ought to say no more, as you must be far too busy at this moment to read long letters; but I think it right to add that, after nearly forty years' editorial experience, in the Old as well as the New World, I have not yet found any daily journal at all equal to your Public Ledger in supplying general and local information to the community, at a price so low that I often wonder how you can afford it. The variety of news, as well as the successful effort to deprive it of that diffuseness which is the crying evil of newspapers at present, the healthy tone, the reliability of the information—*these* are points which strike me, day after day, as a constant reader. No wonder that the public at large appreciate them also.

Very soon after I came to this city, ten years ago, to perform the duties of associate editor of "The Press," then being established by my kind and able friend Mr. Forney, I had the advantage of becoming acquainted with you; an acquaintance which soon matured into mutual regard and friendship. As I recall the vanished years, I recollect your saying to me—it must have been nearly nine years ago—that, *if you lived, you would become proprietor of the Public Ledger;* which the then owners, by the way, had not the remotest idea of parting with. When you fulfilled your prophecy, I was not in the least surprised, for I knew your energy, your persistency, and your enterprise.

With warmest regards, I am, my dear Childs,
Your faithful friend,
R. SHELTON MACKENZIE.

Geo. W. Childs.

[From HORACE GREELEY, Editor of the "New York Tribune."]

ALBANY, June 5, 1867.

DEAR SIR: You may not have observed the fact that I am a member of the Constitutional Convention, now sitting here to revise the Constitution of our State. The duties thus accepted by me will preclude my attendance at your festival. I am sure, however, that it will be amply attended, and that so signal an era in the history of your journal will be fitly and deservedly honored.

Allow me to suggest this sentiment for your festival:

Our National Reconstruction: while it unshackles every slave, may it give no victim to the gallows, but fling open every cell of every political prisoner.

Yours,
HORACE GREELEY.

GEO. W. CHILDS,
   Editor Ledger, Philadelphia.

[From Col. A. J. H. DUGANNE, Editor of the "New York Dispatch."]

ALBANY, June 10, 1867.

MR. GEO. W. CHILDS.

MY DEAR SIR: It would give me much pleasure to be present at the opening of your new building on the 20th inst., but my duties as a member of the convention here in session must forbid. I need not assure you, dear sir, whom personally I esteem so highly, that my best wishes and congratulations will attend the interesting festival; and I beg leave to send you the following toast:—

The Old Paper and the New Building: the former an example of how *Public* a LEDGER may be made, when kept by *Private* Integrity: the latter a symbol of that solid and beautiful *Reputation* which the life of a good citizen erects in the community wherein he dwells.

I remain, very cordially, yours,
A. J. H. DUGANNE.

[From the Hon. WM. BROSS, Lieutenant-Governor of Illinois, and one of the Proprietors and Editors of the "Chicago Tribune."]

ILLINOIS LEGISLATURE SENATE CHAMBER.
SPRINGFIELD, June 15, 1867.

GEO. W. CHILDS.

MY DEAR SIR: I regret exceedingly that my engagements will not permit me to accept your very kind invitation to be present at the formal opening of the NEW LEDGER BUILDING. I regret this the more, as I wish to see for myself the evidences of that splendid success which has crowned your efforts, proving, as it does, that the time has come when the press can be really independent. The conductors of the LEDGER have appreciated that growing intelligence of the American people which now demands the news, and the advocacy of sound political and moral principles, rather than mere devotion to party. The press, not many years ago, was the organ of political cliques; it dared not offend some trickster, whose influence was supposed to be essential to its very existence. Now, its success is assured precisely in the ratio that it adheres to the right and denounces the wrong, no matter who may perpetrate or uphold that wrong. To simplify and make known to the public every new fact in science—to encourage and develop a pure national literature—to illustrate and enforce sound and comprehensive political and moral principles, and, in general, to do all that can be done to cultivate, instruct, and elevate our common humanity, and render it more virtuous, and therefore more prosperous and happy;—these were some of the duties and high prerogatives of the American press. Acting on these principles, no party has money enough to bribe the independent metropolitan press to support false issues and bad men; and hence the charge of venality, so often made against it, is fast becoming an absurdity. Venal presses there still may be, but they are destined to a sure and early extinction. Integrity, energy, commanding talents, comprehensive learning, and perfect independence, now characterize the leading journals of the country, and are the sources of their popularity and power. Among these journals the people recognize the LEDGER; and hence the marked success which is appropriately celebrated by the completion of your magnificent building, and the festivities attending it.

I beg to propose, "The Press"—not only "the palladium of our liberties," but the patron and the defender of everything that can elevate and promote the intelligence, the prosperity, and the happiness of the human family.

Wishing you and your guests all possible happiness, I am, most respectfully and very truly,

Your obedient servant,
WM. BROSS.

[From C. D. BRIGHAM, Editor of the "Pittsburgh Commercial."]

"COMMERCIAL" OFFICE,
PITTSBURGH, June 14, 1867.

MR. GEO. W. CHILDS.

DEAR SIR: A conflict between inclination and a variety of opposing circumstances has delayed my acknowledgment of the receipt of your kind invitation to the LEDGER Opening on the 20th instant. I need not assure you that the inclination has been and is to be present. Nor need I assure you—familiar as you are with editorial life—of the nature of the opposing circumstances. Such conflicts are doubtless familiar to you. In this instance, I have been compelled to forego what, for days, I have contemplated in the light of possibility with genuine pleasure. We all worship success—I do in the newspaper world: and so marked an instance of it as the LEDGER—not only in its present unequalled position, but in its whole history—does not fail to receive my peculiar homage.

Promising myself the satisfaction of a quiet visit to the NEW LEDGER BUILDING "some day," probably about the time Mr. Greeley goes fishing, and thanking you sincerely for your kind invitation, I beg leave to subscribe myself

Yours faithfully,
C. D. BRIGHAM.

[From the Editors and Proprietors of the " Missouri Republican."]

OFFICE OF GEORGE KNAPP & CO.,
" MISSOURI REPUBLICAN," 111 and 113 Chestnut St.
ST. LOUIS, June 7, 1867.

GEO. W. CHILDS.

DEAR SIR: We received to-day your letter of the 3d inst. Please accept our thanks for the friendly terms in which you invite us to be present at the formal opening of the NEW LEDGER BUILDING, which is to take place on the 20th of this month. We are compelled, by reasons of a business and personal character, to deny ourselves the pleasure of meeting you on the occasion named, when we should have the opportunity in person of tendering to you our most hearty congratulations upon the merited success and rare prosperity which have attended your career as a journalist, and upon the splendid contribution which you have made to the facilities of the newspaper art, in the magnificent and costly building which you propose to dedicate on the 20th to the interests of journalism.

While obliged to decline your invitation, we may be permitted to say to you that you present in yourself, and in the grand results you have achieved, an interesting and instructive example of the substantial pecuniary rewards which await a resolute purpose, patient industry, a sagacious, liberal policy in management, a wise public spirit, and high personal honor. These have assured to you surprising and most rapid pecuniary success, with that which we know you value most of all, the confidence and esteem of your fellow-citizens.

Please accept from us expressions of our most cordial good wishes for your continued prosperity, and for the increased popularity of the journal which, through your intelligent direction and control, has won for itself a wide and commanding field of influence, and a most enviable share of popular favor.

Awaiting, with pleasant anticipation, the gratifying reports which we are sure will be given to the public, of the ceremonies and festivities with which the inauguration of the LEDGER BUILDING will be celebrated,

We remain,

Most truly your friends,

GEORGE KNAPP & CO.

[From A. M. HOLBROOK, Esq., Proprietor and Editor of the New Orleans "Picayune."]

OFFICE OF THE "PICAYUNE,"
NEW ORLEANS, June 8, 1867.

GEO. W. CHILDS, Esq.

MY DEAR SIR: Your telegram of the 5th inst., addressed to me, renewing your kind invitation made last summer, to be present at the opening for use of the grand edifice which you have built for your Journal, was duly received; and I have been trying to so fix the disposal of my time that I could be present. Despairing of this, I write to you now to express my deep regret that I shall not be able to be with you.

The LEDGER is a folio whose pages show so many credits to your account, that I cannot, in commensurate terms, declare my admiration of the ability with which it is managed and edited by you. The LEDGER itself, and the great monument to the Art of Arts which you have erected, are in themselves too expressive to need eulogy.

Hoping that you and your guests may enjoy their reunion under your roof tree, I will append a sentiment, which I pray you to repeat to them; and subscribe myself

Your friend and co-worker,

A. M. HOLBROOK.

Philadelphia and its LEDGER—clean, well kept, and well balanced. May they always be as square, and continue to be as crowded, as they now are.

THE PUBLIC LEDGER BUILDING.

[From W. A. Collins, Esq., Editor of the "Pittsburgh Chronicle."]

OFFICE OF THE "EVENING CHRONICLE,"
PITTSBURGH, June 8, 1867.

MR. GEO. W. CHILDS.

DEAR SIR: The absence of my partner on a European tour will prevent either of us accepting your flattering invitation to be present at the opening of the NEW LEDGER BUILDING. I avail myself of this occasion, however, to express a sentiment long cherished, and that is, that the success of the Philadelphia LEDGER demonstrates that wealth and legitimate influence in the newspaper world may be acquired without ministering to gross appetites, pandering to violent prejudices, becoming the vassal of temporarily popular opinions, or in short resorting to any *ad captandum* devices to secure public favor.

The temperate and thoughtful spirit in which the LEDGER discusses questions of exigent interest, its rare abstinence from the jargon and strife of politics, the admirable system of condensation with which it embraces the field of current news, and the refinement and purity of its tone and management considered as a whole, make it, in our judgment, a *type* of what a business, literary, and family journal should be.

In wishing the LEDGER success, we employ only another mode of expressing our sincere desire that the taste of the American people may accept the true and reject the false.

I am, cordially and heartily,
Your well-wisher,
WILLIAM A. COLLINS.

[From Col. John S. Dusolle, Editor of the "New York Sunday Times."]

Office of the "Sunday Times,"
New York, June 8, 1867.

Mr. Geo. W. Childs.

Dear Sir: I have received your polite invitation to assist at the "opening of the New Ledger Building" on the 20th instant, and I accept it with much pleasure. Seventeen years have elapsed since, as the editor of the "Spirit of the Times," I shared in the *esprit du corps* that animated the Press of your city. For over thirteen years of my editorial career in Philadelphia, my sanctum stood *vis-à-vis* to the *old* Ledger Building, and for nearly seven years I enjoyed a cordial intimacy with Mr. Swain, its active manager and your predecessor. Such an experience naturally makes me anxious to see the *new* Ledger Building, its present enterprising proprietor, his aids, &c.

Respectfully yours,
JOHN S. DUSOLLE.

[From S. M. Pettengill, Esq.]

Newspaper Advertising Agency,
New York, June 19, 1867.

Geo. W. Childs.

Dear Sir: I regret that business of importance will prevent my attendance at the opening of the New Ledger Building. Allow me to say that I congratulate you on this new evidence of your prosperity and success. We have always found the Ledger one of the very best newspapers in the country for the advertiser, and always recommend it, as it invariably gives a good return for the money expended in it, and satisfaction to the advertiser.

The Public Ledger: may its balance always be on the right side, as its editor is, and its shadow never be less.

Yours truly,
S. M. PETTENGILL.

[From L. A. Godey, Esq., Editor and Proprietor of the "Lady's Book."]

June 14, 1867.

My Dear Mr. Childs: I accept your kind invitation with great pleasure. I long to meet those who will be present to do you honor, and I know no man who better deserves that honor. The Ledger, under your management, has wonderfully improved in appearance and literary merit, and I know that its circulation has also increased. May it continue to do so, until you cry, " Hold! enough."

Yours, cordially,

L. A. GODEY.

www.ingramcontent.com/pod-product-compliance
Lightning Source LLC
Chambersburg PA
CBHW032144160426
43197CB00008B/772